San Miguel de Allende & Guanajuato

EXPLORER'S GUIDES

San Miguel de Allende & Guanajuato

A Great Destination

Kevin Delgado

SECOND EDITION

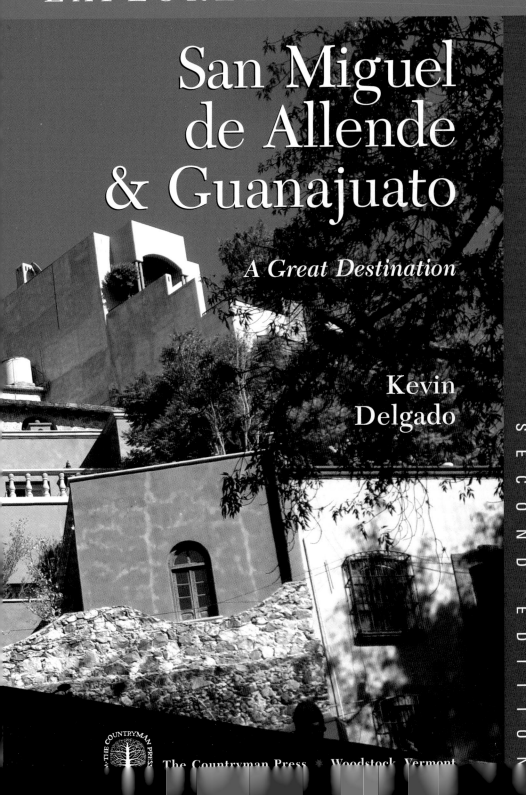

THE COUNTRYMAN PRESS

The Countryman Press * Woodstock, Vermont

Explorer's Guide San Miguel de Allende & Guanajuato: A Great Destination

ISBN: 978-1-58157-131-8

Fronticepiece photo, © Coast to Coast Photography/iStockphoto.com

Interior photographs by the author unless otherwise specified.
Maps by Erin Greb Cartography, © The Countryman Press
Book design by Joanna Bodenweber
Composition by Eugenie S. Delaney

Published by The Countryman Press, P.O. Box 748, Woodstock, VT 05091
Distributed by W. W. Norton & Company, Inc., 500 Fifth Avenue, New York, NY 10110
Printed in the United States of America

10 9 8 7 6 5 4 3 2 1

For my dad.

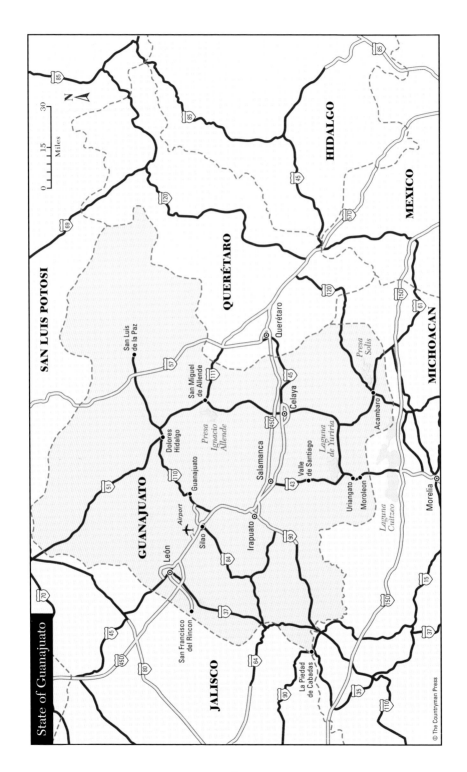

State of Guanajuato

SAN LUIS POTOSI

QUERÉTARO

HIDALGO

MEXICO

MICHOACAN

GUANAJUATO

JALISCO

N

Miles
0   15   30

San Luis
de la Paz

San Miguel
de Allende

Dolores
Hidalgo

Guanajuato

Airport

Silao

León

San Francisco
del Rincon

Irapuato

Salamanca

Querétaro

Celaya

Valle
de Santiago

Uriangato

Moroleon

Acambaro

Presa
Solis

Laguna
de Yuriria

Presa
Ignacio
Allende

Laguna
Cuitzeo

Morelia

La Piedad
de Cabadas

© The Countryman Press

6

Contents

ACKNOWLEDGMENTS 8

INTRODUCTION 11

THE WAY THIS BOOK WORKS 15

HISTORY 19

TRANSPORTATION 49

1. SAN MIGUEL DE ALLENDE 67

2. GUANAJUATO 121

3. SIDE TRIPS 187

4. INFORMATION 205

INDEX 231

MAPS

State of Guanajuato 6

City of San Miguel de Allende 73

City of Guanajuato 122

Guanajuato Historic Center 167

Guanajuato Churches 178

City of Dolores Hidalgo 188

Cañada de la Virgen Excursion 201

Acknowledgments

THERE IS A BLACK AND WHITE PICTURE on my sister's living room wall of a dark, mustachioed man in the round straw hat of a farmworker. He is not smiling, nor does he look as though he has much of a sense of humor. However, I cannot help but smile every time I look at the picure. He is my grandfather, and that picture is one of the very few of him that exist. He was a shoemaker from Guanajuato who, against all common sense, uprooted his family from the only land they ever knew and trudged them north in search of a better life. It was an arduous journey, and at times extremely tragic, but after many years he found a new home in a cinder block shack along a dirt road in southeastern Wyoming. My older brothers and sisters would tell stories about him in his later years; how he would walk along that dirt road where, by that time, many of his children had also settled, and his grandchildren would run out to meet him. He didn't speak much English and his grandkids didn't speak much Spanish, but they were always happy to see him and he always seemed to have chewing gum ready to hand out. Unfortunately, I never met my grandfather—but I always felt a certain connection to that picture. Perhaps it is his strong resemblance to my father, or the stories told to me by my aunts. But when I was older I traveled to Guanajuato with a sense of anticipation, and found I could not walk along its streets without thinking of my grandpa. I still walk along the streets looking for that stern face in the people I pass, and it makes me smile. This book is for my grandparents and their children—Aunt Lupe, Aunt Dolores, Uncle John, Aunt Sadie, Uncle Joe, Aunt Francis, Aunt Isabel, Aunt Rose, Uncle Tony, and, of course, my dad.

I am forever in the debt of the cast of characters whose stories and insights have contributed to this book. Thanks especially to Mike

Brady for all the rides to and from the border and for all the travel and photography advice. Thanks to John Harten, Greg Zsulgit, and the other Yampounding Sherpas, for your wisdom and for dragging me along on all those adventures. I am thankful for the kindness, support, and assistance of the hoteliers, restaurant owners, tour operators, and others whom I visited during my research. Thank you to Betty, Monica, and Robert, as well as to Penny and Todd for keeping an eye on the kids—and to Daniel, Summer, Riley, and Isabel for your patience; to my parents, for always giving me a chance; to my brothers and sisters (Mickey, D. J., Lori, Barbie, Davie, Teddy, Brian, Penny, Darren, Ryan, and Sean), for making me who I am; to my old buddy, Brian Schwartzkopf; to Mona Klausing, just for being there; and, notably, thank you Simon Lozano and Craig Sodaro for teaching me to write. And, of course, thank you Mary, for all you do for me.

Introduction

WHEN MOST PEOPLE THINK about a Mexican vacation, an image immediately comes to mind. You're sitting under an umbrella on a white sand beach and looking out over a crystal blue sea, while sipping on a margarita that was just served to you by the same guy that carried your luggage to your room yesterday and served you breakfast today. That Mexico exists in many places along the Pacific Coast, the Yucatán Peninsula, and very near the spot where you may have taken this book off the shelf at your local bookstore. This book isn't about that Mexico. This is about the state of Guanajuato, which is completely landlocked by a bunch of other landlocked states (well, Michoacán isn't completely landlocked, but you get the point). Moreover, it is not a place where you will find very many brand-name hotels, and there are none at the center of the action. You will also not find any all-inclusive resorts with 24-hour buffets, or familiar fast food restaurants. In short, this book is about a place that is likely outside your normal comfort zone. No need to fret, however. In San Miguel de Allende, Guanajuato, and Dolores Hidalgo, you will find towns that are extremely safe and full of people who will welcome you as their guest and proudly show you the wonders of their cities. And there are wonders.

Even if you live along the East Coast of the United States or Canada, you probably see very few buildings that are more than a couple hundred years old—and those that are old are likely surrounded by structures that were put up much more recently. However, a walk along the cobblestone streets of these Central Mexican towns is a rare journey in North America, because you are surrounded by

LEFT: Guanajuato is honeycombed with narrow alleys. Maria Miller Kisska

11

A brass band entertains in Jardín de la Unión.

entire blocks that exist much as they did in the 17th and 18th centuries. And while the residents of these towns have done much over the last century to preserve their historic treasures, it was a tumultuous and complicated course of events that allowed the buildings to survive into the 21st century.

Early on in the history of Spanish colonization, San Miguel de Allende became a fashionable place to live for the wealthy families of Central Mexico. The investment that these families put into their town can be seen all over the central district of that city today. As for Guanajuato, the vast wealth from massive veins of silver discovered in the surrounding hills fueled the investment in infrastructure that made this city one of the jewels of colonial Mexico. However, the good times didn't last. Political instability, war, and economic hardship in effect froze these cities in time. For a while many of Guanajuato's great architectural works fell into disrepair, with one of its churches sitting in rubble for decades—while San Miguel de Allende was all but abandoned. On the other hand, Dolores Hidalgo came to be known as *la cuna de la independencia*, or "the cradle of the independence," because it was here in 1810 that the priest Miguel Hidalgo struck the first blow for independence from Spain. An interest in this history, as well as better times, brought rejuvenation to the region. And the beauty of its towns has been widely recognized. The entire town of San Miguel de Allende is a national monument, and Guanajuato is recognized as a world heritage site.

However, Mexico is peppered with beautiful colonial cities, where you can blow in for a few hours and wander around admiring the architecture before hitching the next bus to the beach. These cities are much more than that. They are worth a visit not because of the life that went on here hundreds of years ago, but rather because of the life that is happening in them today. San Miguel de Allende is today a Mecca for artists, musicians, chefs, and creative people from around the world. In fact, they don't just come here to visit, they come to settle down. In fact, it is home to upward of five thousand American and Canadian expatriates who have come here to study art, start businesses, and retire. The town is an artists' colony with galleries all over the central district. You will find live music just about any night of the week, and restaurants serving cuisine from all over the world. An hour and a half away in the town of Guanajuato, you will find a city that is equally as vibrant, with a little green heart that beats to the rhythm of mariachi and Spanish *estudiantina* music. This little green heart is known as the Jardín de la Unión, a wedge-shaped square lined with low Indian laurel trees and outdoor cafés. This square is the scene of constant activity and a mix of young university students, foreign travelers, and well-to-do locals. A walk in any direction will lead you to another café-lined plaza, and the fact that the town is built in a steep valley with traffic flowing through a series of narrow underground tunnels means that walking is just about the most efficient way to get around. A detour through any of the town's numerous alleys is almost certain to let out into a plaza, where you will find still more people sitting at outdoor cafés enjoying the beautiful Central Mexican weather.

To top it all off, these towns are also famous for their many annual festivals, which draw visitors from throughout Mexico and from around the world. This is particularly true during Holy Week, and in the fall when the streets around the historic centers become crowded with merrymakers and vendors of all types. Yes, a trip to San Miguel de Allende, Guanajuato, or Dolores Hidalgo may take you out of your comfort zone, but what you will find once you're there is a world filled with the cultural wonders—sights, sounds, and tastes—that only Mexico can provide.

The Way This Book Works

THIS BOOK IS DIVIDED into four chapters covering specific regions of the central Mexican state of Guanajuato. Recommendations and reviews cover a range of options that vary in style and price; they will help you to make decisions—whether you are staying in one area or intend to travel the region.

Some entries, most notably those in the Pick Your Spot (lodging) and Local Flavors (dining) sections of chapters, include information (telephone, Web site) at the beginning of each listing. All such information has been checked for accuracy as close to the time of publication as possible, but things change, so it's best to check in advance. Wherever possible I have included Web sites for you to find up-to-date prices, menus, and room options—as well as where to find the establishment's social media presence. The best of the sites provide creative and useful links to local blogs. For year-round tourist information and seasonal activities, see the Information chapter.

PRICES

Lodging in San Miguel de Allende tends to be more expensive than in any other colonial city in this region of Mexico. Anything under $120 per night here would be considered inexpensive, while moderate prices run up to around $200 per night. Anything more than that should be considered expensive, even by San Miguel standards. By contrast, lodging in Guanajuato for around $90 per night or less would be inexpensive—though you can certainly find adequate lodging for $50 per night or less even at the city center (if you don't mind

LEFT: Street stands offer a quick snack when you're on the go.

There are many galleries to choose from in San Miguel de Allende.

a no frills room). Moderate rates in Guanajuato run up to about $150 per night, and anything over that should be considered expensive. Rates tend to go up a bit during the high tourist season of December 15 to April 1, when days are sunny and clear and nights are crisp and cool. However, during festivals such as Cerventino, Semana Santa, and the week after Christmas, prices go up rather dramatically. That said, the rates in this colonial enclave are still much more reasonable than you will find in Mexico City or in the resort towns on the Pacific.

Price Codes

San Miguel de Allende

	LODGING	DINING
Inexpensive	Up to $120	Up to $7
Moderate	$120 to $200	$7 to $12
Expensive	Over $200	$12 to $30 and above

Guanajuato

	LODGING	DINING
Inexpensive	$50 to $90	Up to $7
Moderate	$90 to $150	$7 to $12
Expensive	Over $150	$12 to $30 and above

History

GUANAJUATO IS THE CENTER OF MEXICO both geographically and culturally. A landlocked state in the heart of the Mexican Republic, it shares borders with San Luis Potosí and Zacatecas on the north, Querétaro on the east, the state of México on the southeast, Jalisco on the west, and Michoacán on the south. It is a relatively small state in terms of territory. With just over 19,000 square miles, it ranks 22nd among Mexico's 31 states. However, its cultural and geographical importance is undeniable.

When Spanish conquistadores arrived in Mexico in the 16th century, this territory was a backwater populated by bands of hunter-gatherer tribes. However, it was relatively close to Tenóchtitlan, the capital of the Aztecs—the most powerful indigenous tribe on the continent. Had Europeans arrived at the height of the Toltec or Mayan empires, Mexican geography would likely look much different today. However, the Spanish made the former Aztec capital their base of operations in New Spain, from which to set about conquering the continent. Trade routes to the northern territories ran through Guanajuato, making the early settlement of San Miguel el Grande (which became San Miguel de Allende) an important stopover. Furthermore, Spanish explorers quickly discovered rich veins of silver in the mountains surrounding the present-day city of Guanajuato.

The economic activities that sprung from these circumstances led to a particularly independent streak among the residents of San

LEFT: The Parroquia de San Miguel towers over the city's main plaza.

The state of Guanajuato has produced many notable figures, including the artist Diego Rivera, singer José Alfredo Jiménez, and former president Vicente Fox.

Miguel, Guanajuato, and other nearby settlements. This important factor led to a local movement that culminated in Mexico's independence from Spain in the early 19th century. This region has also been home to many of Mexico's most notable figures, including the artist Diego Rivera, singer José Alfredo Jiménez, and former president Vicente Fox.

Guanajuato is one of those places where the history is apparent wherever you look. From the beautiful colonial houses along San Miguel's avenues, to the mines of Guanajuato, to the statue of Hidalgo in the center of the town square in Dolores Hidalgo—this place values its history and is eager to help you experience it for yourself.

NATURAL HISTORY

San Miguel de Allende and the town of Guanajuato are located in the central plateau of Mexico in a geographical region known as *El Bajío*, or lowlands, which includes the low mountains of Sierra de Guanajuato and the plains to the south. While this region is primarily known for its unquestionable historic significance, its many monuments, and cultural festivals, it also has a wealth of natural beauty. This aspect of the region tends to be overshadowed by fiestas and architecture, but visitors wanting to get away from the bustle of the tourist centers can find serene moments in the undeveloped areas along rustic mountain paths, or along the many springs that lie just outside of San Miguel de Allende.

This area of *El Bajío* lies along a transitional geographic zone between the plains and the mountains, as well as between the fertile basin of the Lerma River and the deserts that open to the north. Because of this varied geography, this region possesses a variety of important natural resources that are both beautiful and vital to the Mexican economy.

The Laja River Basin

The Laja River, an important tributary of the Lerma River, lies to the west of the city of San Miguel de Allende. This tributary, fed by the waters of the mountain ranges north of Guanajuato state, flows from north to south into a reservoir bottled up by the Don Ignacio Allende Dam, an enormous hydraulic structure just to the southwest of San Miguel that was inaugurated in 1967. The banks of the Laja River were the principal site of pre-Hispanic settlements in the region. In

Guanajuato is located on a plateau in Mexico's Bajio region.

the 16th century, Franciscan monks also used this river as a route from the south by which to penetrate into the lands of the Chichimecas. The first foundation of the town of San Miguel also took place right on the banks of the Laja River, in an area with abundant springs. Today, several old chapels that were built by early converted indigenous people still survive along the Laja, as well as the ruins of one-time haciendas and demolished bridges and aqueducts.

Some of these early buildings, as well as Chichimeca ruins, lie submersed beneath the waters of the Don Ignacio Allende Dam. Despite the loss of heritage sites that this dam has caused, today it provides ample recreational space for sailing, fishing, and other water sports for San Miguel residents. At the same time, it has gradually been transformed into a refuge for a variety of aquatic and migratory birds (many of which are endangered) such as herons, ibis, pelicans, and wild ducks.

Above the Laja River basin, between the famous sanctuary of Atotonílco and the Don Ignacio Allende Dam, is a cluster of springs and wells that the area's rural communities have relied on for centuries. Additionally, these springs have given life to a wide diversity of flora and fauna. Dense stands of reeds border marshes and streams formed by the springs, together with thick gatherings of mesquite—called "the tree of life" by the Chichimecas due to its great value as lumber, food, and medicine. This forested region is home to many populations of multicolored birds such as blue grosbeaks, vermilion flycatchers, and great kiskadees.

Los Picachos Mountain Range

In the town of San Miguel de Allende, these are the mountains clearly visible if one gazes off to the southeast. For hundreds of years they have provided an important source of water for the surrounding communities. The peaks and canyons of these mountains are covered with thick woods, predominantly composed of oak. In fact, as many as seven varieties of oak create shelter for a diverse natural ecosystem here. It has managed to survive thanks in great part to the region's relative isolation from the runaway urban development that has taken place in areas such as Mexico City and Guadalajara.

However, since the 16th century the forested surface of the region has been drastically reduced through overgrazing, fires, and

Cerro de la Bufa just outside the town of Guanajuato.

The city of Guanajuato is located in the foothills of Los Picachos mountain range.

indiscriminate deforestation for lumber and firewood. The gradual loss of this vegetative cover and the excessive drilling of wells, principally for farming, have contributed to the desertification of the area. Overdrilling has also lowered the water table in general, and specifically caused the disappearance of many of the springs that have been so important to the area.

However, today the mountain range of Los Picachos is a protected area, along with other nearby woodlands and ravines, such as La Márgara to the east and La Cañada de la Virgen (the Glen of the Virgin) to the west. In 1989 a territorial reserve of more than 200 acres,

La Cañada de los Pajaritos, was set aside for the preservation of woodlands. Its name comes from a species of large blue birds, which abound here in noisy flocks among the oak groves. Other species that can be found here include eagles, coyotes, red fox, and white-tailed deer, which have managed to avoid extermination despite the activities of the poachers that have unfortunately operated here since it became a reserve.

Travelers looking for some outdoor fun can climb to La Cañada de los Pajaritos and return to San Miguel in the same day with relative ease. If you are interested in overnight adventures you can camp in the reserve, which is equipped with several shelters. From the heights of Los Picachos you will find a magnificent panoramic view in all directions.

Guanajuato Semidesert

At the time of the conquest, the area that is now San Miguel de Allende and Guanajuato was likely covered with temperate woodlands. Soon after, however, the process of deforestation began to result in a wide-ranging ecological change to a semiarid environment that today characterizes the region.

Calcareous and sandy soils have sustained an astonishing variety of cacti—including spiny *garambullo*, agaves valued for making tequila, yuccas with sword-shaped leaves, "spoon plants," and prickly pear *nopales*. The majority of these desert plants flower majestically during the spring, when regular rainfall results in a carpet of multicolored flowers. Other plant species that have managed to survive here include mesquite, acacia, and morning glory. This flora comes together to create the classic image of the rural countryside of the Mexican high plateau, with rolling hills covered in grasslands, sparse trees, and cacti.

The foothills around San Miguel are also scarred by numerous deep and craggy ravines that slash the hills, mesas, and semidesert prairies of the surrounding countryside. These ravines also shelter their own variety of flora and fauna. Even aquatic plants grow in small pools of water shaded by native trees such as mulberry, copal, and walnut. The ravines also provide an ecological niche for several types of native birds, foxes, badgers, and armadillos. Unfortunately, like much of the rest of the area's natural beauty, these microhabitats are threatened by hunting, overgrazing, and deforestation. These ravines formed at the foot of the Los Picachos Mountain Range—

particularly the area of La Cañada de la Virgen, 30 miles southwest of San Miguel de Allende. This is also the location of a rare archaeological site. Closer to San Miguel, El Charco del Ingenio Botanical Gardens presents another example of the natural beauty you will find here. This site contains 135 acres of ravines set aside for the preservation of the region's ecological treasures. It is run by a nongovernmental group dedicated to restoring microhabitats and promoting the conservation of Guanajuato's natural resources.

These natural resources are plentiful. Despite the fact that Guanajuato does not have the white sand beaches of Cancún and Cabo, it does have plenty of natural beauty. Moreover, it is a beauty you can

Guanajuato is home to a wide variety of plant life.

Don Ignacio Allende is a deeply important figure in Mexican history.

enjoy in peace and contemplation, so you are well rested when you are ready to return to your world.

Cultural History

Guanajuato is undeniably one of the most culturally and historically important regions in Mexico. For a place with no significant indigenous ruins, that is really saying something. However, when you walk the streets of Guanajuato, you are walking in the footsteps of Diego Rivera. When you stand in the town square of Dolores Hidalgo, you can almost hear the voice of Hidalgo himself calling out *El Grito* for the first time. And when you stare up at the Parroquia in San Miguel de Allende, you see the radical vision of Zeferino Gutiérrez as he conceived of a majestic church by looking at a postcard. But more than these famous examples, Guanajuato represents the iconic image of the small Mexican village with towering churches, open squares, grizzled expatriates, and peasant farmers leading their burros through town. Incredibly, to this day you will still find all of this while wandering along the streets of Guanajuato's towns.

Before the arrival of the Spanish conquistadores in the 16th century, the region of Mexico where San Miguel de Allende and Guanajuato are located was populated by several small bands of indigenous people who lived a nomadic way of life. At that time, these groups depended on hunting and gathering for their survival. These indigenous tribes made note of the numerous frogs in the area and referred to it as *Quanax-juato*, meaning "Place of Frogs," the sound of which the Spanish would translate to "Guanajuato." Although all of these groups are today commonly referred to as Chichimecas, there were actually ethnically distinct groups with names such as Cazacanes, Guamares, Copuces, and Guachichiles. The ancient Aztecs were the first to refer to these groups as Chichimecas, a pejorative term that implied that they descended from dogs. The Spaniards would use the word as an umbrella term to describe most of the indigenous groups scattered through large parts of Guanajuato, Jalisco, Zacatecas, San Luis Potosí, Aguascalientes, and Durango.

Pre-Hispanic art on display at the Alhóndiga Museum in Guanajuato.

However, the culture of this region had not always been limited to small groups of hunter-gatherers. Populations closely connected to the advanced Mesoamerican cultures to the south occupied Guanajuato many centuries earlier. These early populations were organized into small communities that settled along the banks of the Laja River between A.D. 950 and 1110, and spread out around most of what is today the state of Guanajuato. These societies were linked by trade to the ancient city of Tula and the great metropolis of Teotihuacán, located just north of present day Mexico City (not to be confused with the Aztec capital of Tenóchtitlan). Moreover, there is evidence to suggest that this region was actually the northwestern frontier of the Toltec empire. Around the year A.D. 1100, agricultural practices seem to have ceased almost completely in Guanajuato, and by 1200 the urban centers of the region had been abandoned. The desertion of the northern provinces of the Toltec empire was due to a political power struggle between the followers of the feathered serpent god Quetzalcóatl and the Tezcatipoca, who ruled in the Toltec capital of Tula. This political strife was compounded by an extended drought in this region, which provoked a mass migration out of Guanajuato to the central high plateau in Michoacán. As the great Mesoamerican cultures shifted to the southwest, Guanajuato was inhabited by more primitive migratory groups. Over the next 300 years, little changed in the way these groups went about their lives.

Sowing the Seeds of San Miguel

In 1521, after a bloody struggle between the Aztecs and the Spaniards led by Hernán Cortés, the Aztec capital city of Tenóchtitlan fell to the conquistadores, becoming the capital of New Spain and a base from which the Spanish conquistadors could conquer the rest of Mexico and beyond. However, even after the subjugation of Mexico's indigenous peoples, the Spaniards had to struggle arduously against native traditions, particularly with regards to religious practices. The exploration and colonization of the state of Guanajuato was initiated from the region of Michoacán to the southwest.

The first settlement in Guanajuato was the monastery of San Francisco de Acámbaro, established near the Lerma River on September 19, 1526, by monks from the town of Urúapan, Michoacán. From this location, Spanish missionaries set out to explore the Chichimeca lands to the north. In 1542, the Franciscan Friar Juan de San Miguel, from the monastery of Acámbaro, set out to the north

The city of San Miguel de Allende predates any settlement in the United States.

along the Grande River and its tributaries on an expedition that explored as far as the Laja River. He intended to find an appropriate location to establish a town in the region in order to serve as a center of catechization of the local indigenous population. This expedition led him to the upper basin of the Laja River, where he constructed a small church called the Chapel of San Miguel Viejo and a small settlement called San Miguel de los Chichimecas. He left this settlement in the hands of his associate, Friar Bernardo Cossin, who struggled for years to convert the Copuces, one of the most violent indigenous groups in the region. Catholicism proved a difficult sell to the Copuces and in 1551 they set fire to the settlement, forcing the friar to find a new location from which to preach. He chose a spot several kilometers away, situated just above a slope that provided for better defenses. This location also contained a spring that would provide fresh water for the new settlement, which he called San Miguel el Grande. Today, this location is occupied by San Miguel de Allende, and the spring continues to provide water to the city.

The first building that Friar Bernardo Cossin raised on his new site was the Chapel of La Santa Cruz, which was located near the spring. The town of San Miguel el Grande gradually grew around the chapel, populated by groups of indigenous people coming from around Central Mexico. Today, this old section of San Miguel, located on the southeast edge of town, is known as the Quarter of El Chorro.

Early Economic Development

Beginning around 1550, the sparse Chichimeca populations in the territory of Guanajuato began to be displaced by indigenous groups from other parts of Mexico, such as Tarascans from Michoacán, Otomies from Querétaro, and Mexicas from the Mexico City region. These immigrants came to work on the cattle ranches in the area. As a result of the influx of migratory populations, the town of San Miguel el Grande and the surrounding area experienced a diversification of its workforce. The population that settled in San Miguel el Grande possessed skills in working with textiles and metals.

A statue of a Mexíca warrior at the Museo de la Independéncia Nacional in Dolores Hidalgo.

In 1555, Viceroy Don Luis de Velasco decided to invest in the development of the town of San Miguel el Grande in order to defend access roads leading to Zacatecas and San Luis Potosí, where silver and gold were already being mined. On his urging, 50 Spanish families relocated to the area, constructing a new settlement just to the north of the Quarter of El Chorro. In 1564, the Chapel of San Rafael was established on this site by Don Vasco de Quiroga. Its main plaza was situated on the spot where Plaza Civica is today located.

Throughout the rest of the 16th century and into the 17th century, Spanish monks and ranchers continued to colonize the territory of Guanajuato. The lands north of San Miguel el Grande were ideal for raising cattle, and in 1573 Viceroy Don Luis de Velasco granted vast

This region of Mexico retains aspects of bygone eras.

swaths of land in the region of Guanajuato to several Spaniards for the purpose of establishing ranches. These land grants proved to be great sources of wealth for the families that received them, as well as fundamental in the economic development of the fertile plateau of northern Mexico in the 18th century. They sowed the seeds for the large cattle-raising trade that became a well-respected way of life and produced Mexico's famous *jinetes,* or horsemen.

In the 17th century, the discovery and development of the Real de Minas of Santa Fe in Guanajuato created a new source of wealth in the area. At the time, the Spanish crown was engaged in war with other European powers, which weakened its ability to maintain economic relationships with New Spain. As exchanges between New Spain and the mother country decreased, the region of Guanajuato went through an economic and social reorganization, making it more self-sufficient. During this time, the town of San Miguel el Grande enjoyed a long respite from its obligations to the crown, resulting in political and economic power shifting to wealthy local families. The town was located adjacent to the zone that the colonial administration had designated to support the Real de Minas of Santa Fe in Guanajuato. The mines in Guanajuato made local cattle ranchers even more wealthy because, in addition to being agricultural powerhouses, their animals were now needed to provide a source of labor in the mines. Both cattle ranching and mining reached their peak in Guanajuato in the 18th century.

That the land in the territory of Guanajuato was ideal for agriculture—as well as its being centrally located between Zacatecas, Durango, and Mexico City—made the region an important resource throughout the 17th century. Furthermore, this region quickly became one of the largest producers of wheat in New Spain, making it the breadbasket of Mexico. The fields of Acámbaro, Celaya, Salamanca, Silao, and León became the most cultivated in all of New Spain. Wheat farming and corn cultivation was so prosperous that Guanajuato was often referred to as the granary of New Spain.

However, in the latter half of the 18th century silver mining became Guanajuato's main source of economic activity. The deposits of silver discovered in Guanajuato gave rise to an increase in commercial routes through the territory—north to Santa Fe and San Luis Potosí, and west to Guadalajara. San Miguel el Grande was located at the center of this activity and became the focal point mining products, farming products, and manufactured products passed through.

A cobblestone street in Guanajuato.

Guanajuato's historic center is crowded with impressive structures.

Glory Years

In the 17th and 18th centuries, San Miguel el Grande was the residence of choice for many large landholders of Central Mexico. These rich Spaniards and Creoles left their mark on San Miguel, distinguishing it from other towns throughout the region by investing in local architecture and works of art. By 1750, San Miguel el Grande was home to one of the most prosperous populations in all of New Spain. Its city planners were forward thinkers, laying the town out in a checkerboard configuration with ordered streets and blocks of regular shapes and size. The more wealthy residents of San Miguel el Grande built baroque-style homes and churches at the city center around the main square—the Plaza Mayor. The outskirts of town would have been peppered with simple adobe huts that served as residences of the Indians and *mestizos* (mixed race individuals). In terms of local businesses, the town contained several grocery stores, bakeries, and granaries. Owners of these shops were generally wealthy Creoles of Spanish heritage, and some were tied to the commercial monopolies managed by powerful interests in Mexico City.

In 1741, Guanajuato was granted the title of City by King Philip V of Spain. In 1786, New Spain was divided into 12 *intendencias*, one of which was the Intendencia de Guanajuato, with an area about the size of the present-day State of Guanajuato. By this time Guanajuato had become known for a broad range of products, such as ironwork and woolen goods. The excellence of textiles from this region, combined with efficient production techniques, made Guanajuato one of the largest centers for the production of textile goods in New Spain. In particular, the town of San Miguel el Grande became known for its high-quality saddles. This success also meant that San Miguel was developing into an autonomous regional economic power far removed from political influences in Mexico City and the Spanish crown. This fact would be a key factor in the development of Guanajuato as the focal point of the Mexican struggle for independence from Spain. For its part, Guanajuato was the most important silver-producing city in the world. The Valenciana Mine, located just outside the city of Guanajuato, was one of the richest silver finds in history. In the 18th century, this mine alone accounted for 60 percent of the world's total silver production. For this reason, Guanajuato flourished as the silver mining capital of the world for three centuries, producing nearly a third of the world's silver during this time.

Birthplace of Independence

In the late 18th century, Spain had once again turned its attention o its territories across the Atlantic, and was attempting to regain control of the American colonies by enacting more stringent administrative rules—and by pressing for a higher percentage of economic resources. King Carlos III enacted what became known as the Bourbon Reforms, which were a series of measures designed to restrain the autonomy and power of local authorities and interests in New Spain.

In 1762, tensions with the English caused Spain to reorganize the military in its American territories. In order to guarantee loyalty, the crown initially sent continental forces to serve in New Spain. However, maintaining what were essentially foreign forces in its American territories put further strain on the already-stretched Spanish treasury. Therefore, Spain was eventually forced to pare down the number of Spanish troops in New Spain and to use them instead to train forces made up of Creoles. In San Miguel el Grande, financial contributions for military training by the local populace were so great that

Mexican Independence began on the steps of Parroquia de Nuestra Señora de los Dolores in Dolores Hidalgo.

the town was granted its own provincial regiment, known as the Dragoons of the Queen.

In September 1810, tension between the Spanish crown and the colonial establishment had brought Mexico to the cusp of revolution. Spanish forces in the city of Querétaro learned of a conspiracy for independence in the town of Dolores, 25 miles north of San Miguel. As they prepared to take action, the wife of Querétaro's mayor sent word to the insurgents that danger was on its way. The messenger was a member of the Dragoons of the Queen named Don Ignacio Allende. A native son of San Miguel, he had become sympathetic to the Mexican independence movement and had attended secret meetings in Querétaro. He had secretly agreed to be a leader of the independence, should insurgency ever come to fruition. At midnight on September 16, Miguel Hidalgo, the parish priest in Dolores, rang the church bell and called for followers to take up arms and go with him to San Miguel. Soon a group of around seven hundred farmers, miners, and peasants left Dolores armed only with pickaxes and machetes. They stopped in the village of Atotonílco to gather more followers and a cloth with the picture of the Virgin of Guadalupe, the patron saint of Mexico. Afterward, Hidalgo marched through the streets of San Miguel carrying the standard of Guadelupe and leading an army of five thousand. Seeing the insurgents, the mayor of San Miguel immediately turned over the city to Father Hidalgo. This priest had envisioned a bloodless revolution in which the will of the people would overwhelm the powers-that-be throughout Mexico, just as they had in San Miguel. Instead, he would lose his life within months. As for Allende, he quickly became one of the leaders of the rebellion—before being captured and executed in the city of

Miguel Hidalgo is considered the father of Mexico.

Chihuahua. The severed heads of Hidalgo and Allende, along with two other insurgents (Aldama and Jiménez), were brought back to the town of Guanajuato and hung in cages on the Alhóndiga building for the duration of the war. Quickly, Mexico's War for Independence became a bloody class struggle, with the wealthy pitted against the poor, that dragged on for the next 11 years.

Years of Turbulence

Of course, the cause of Allende and Hidalgo did culminate in Mexico's independence from Spain. In 1824, the first Mexican constitution created the sovereign state of Guanajuato with the town of Guanajuato as its capital. The first governor, Carlos Montes de Oca, was a dedicated supporter of education in the state. He was the force behind the reopening of the original College of the Most Holy Trinity, founded by the Jesuits, and the old College of the Immaculate Conception, run by Oratorian priests. The latter was to become the State College of Guanajuato. Despite the fact that the 19th century was a politically unstable period in Mexico, the citizens of Guanajuato managed several important developments in the region. Dams and aqueducts were constructed to serve San Miguel and other towns, and an abundant amount of spring water allowed the urban zone to flourish. Local craft traditions continued to develop and a few industries, such as textiles and masonry, infused some life into local economies. On January 17, 1858, President Benito Juárez temporarily established the capital of the Mexican Republic in the city of Guanajuato, due to the constant persecution leveled against him by conservative factions. Later, during the period of the French Intervention, a garrison of French troops occupied the city of Guanajuato and the newly installed Emperor Maximilian of Hapsburg visited the city in September 1864. It was he who ordered the conversion of the Alhóndiga de Granaditas into a prison.

The final decades of the 19th century were a time of increased development for the region. Foreign investors arrived and pumped money into mines, railways, tramways, telephones, electricity, public lighting, and public spaces such as the La Paz square and statue, Juarez Theater, and the Hidalgo Market. In San Miguel, this developing prosperity manifested itself in public and private works that modernized and beautified the city, though in many cases it was at the

The streets of Guanajuato are largely unchanged from a century ago.

Don Ignacio Allende—Hero of the Independence

José Ignacio María de Allende y Unzaga was born in San Miguel el Grande on January 21, 1769. The son of a wealthy, landed Spanish father (Domingo Narciso de Allende) and a Creole mother (María Ana de Unzaga), Allende attended the prestigious school of San Francisco de Sales with Juan José Martínez de los Reyes, also known by the nickname of *El Pípila*. After graduation in 1795, Allende joined the Dragoons of the Queen as a lieutenant. The military exercises of the Dragoons were limited to drills and guard duty. However, in 1804, tensions between Spain and England began to rise and colonial troops were put on a heightened state of alert to protect against a possible English attack. This situation caused Allende's company to be transferred first to Mexico City and then to Veracruz. Along the way, Allende had a political awakening in which he became convinced it was time for Mexico to vie for independence from Spain. He returned to San Miguel at the end of 1808 and began attending secret insurgent meetings at various locations around the state of Guanajuato. In fact, Allende himself presided over several such meetings that were disguised as mere social gatherings, to hide their intentions from local authorities.

In September 1810, Spanish authorities in Querétaro learned of a burgeoning independence movement in the small town of Dolores, near San Miguel el Grande, and resolved to crush it. What these authorities did not know was that Allende had already agreed to lead the independence movement. As the authorities prepared to move on the conspirators, Allende rushed to Dolores, where the parish priest Miguel Hidalgo had been organizing a small independence movement. After several hours of heated debate, Hidalgo, Allende, and their associates decided it was time to take up arms against the Spanish.

In the early morning hours of September 16, 1810, the insurgents set out from the parish church in Dolores and headed toward San Miguel. Instead of offering resistance, the majority of residents of San Miguel joined the insurgency. Allende was able to convince his fellow soldiers in the regiment of the Dragoons to join the cause, and his influence helped convince San Miguel's

Painting of Don Ignacio Allende displayed in his home in San Miguel de Allende

populace to back the insurgency. The insurgents locked up the Spanish authorities in the school of San Francisco de Sales and quickly named new town authorities. Then, on the morning of September 19, they set out to expand their movement.

After the capture of the Alhóndiga de Granaditas in Guanajuato—the battle that made *El Pípila* famous—Allende decided to march on Mexico City. The insurgents were decimated at the Battle of the Bridge of Calderón, and Allende reversed course—marching north, where he was captured in an ambush. He was taken to the city of Chihuahua where he was tried for insubordination and executed by firing squad on June 26, 1811. His corpse was decapitated and his head was taken back to Guanajuato where it was put on display at the Alhóndiga de Granaditas. In 1824, his remains were buried in the cathedral in Mexico City with honors reserved for viceroys and presidents. Two years later, the name of his hometown was renamed in his honor, from San Miguel el Grande to San Miguel de Allende. In 1925, his remains were moved once again to the Independence column in Mexico City.

expense of destroying 18th-century baroque buildings. It was in these years that the indigenous architect Zeferino Gutiérrez embarked on radical modifications of the baroque facades of the Parroquia and the adjacent church called La Santa Escuela, the clock tower in the heart of the city, and Las Monjas dome of the Iglesia de la Concepción (Church of the Conception). Basing these works on Gothic models, it is said that he was inspired by the images of European churches that adorned the postage stamps and postcards that were arriving in Mexico from Spain at that time. Additionally, other public spaces were modified in those years. The traditional open and paved Hispanic Plaza de Armas was converted to the Jardín Principal with its manicured trees and walkways, as it exists today.

This new age of prosperity in Guanajuato was short-lived, and left in its wake a further centralization of political power in the landed elite as well as increased authoritarianism and decreased social equality. Civil war broke out throughout Mexico in 1910 with the Mexican Revolution. Political instability and uncertainty ended Guanajuato's mining boom, and San Miguel's prosperity once again went into a state of decline. Though these two towns kept themselves at the edge of the revolutionary conflict, they did not escape the constant incursions by military troops traveling to and from such revolutionary hotspots as León, just a few miles away. Many of San Miguel's wealthier families withdrew to safer cities; the working class drifted away, faced with hardship from the decline of the haciendas and of commerce—joining the ranks of armed bands or making their way toward the safety of the United States. Guanajuato lost more than 20 percent of its population—in San Miguel, a remote location and dwindling resources had resulted in a town on the verge of abandonment. Other nearby towns such as Mineral de la Luz did indeed become ghost towns.

This time, though, the decline and depopulation was more gradual than it had been a hundred years before. However, Guanajuato's stability took another hit in 1926 when stringent anticleric laws were put into place by President Plutarco Elías Calles (founder of the PRI political party). These laws resulted in the violent guerilla conflict known as the Cristero War. Being the staunchly Catholic region that it is, Guanajuato was one of the areas that most strongly opposed the new laws, and many battles were fought here.

There is a legend that says that the visitor that drinks from the springs of El Chorro is destined to return someday. This legend is used to explain how San Miguel has continued to bounce back from decline and stagnation time after time. By the late 1920s, the region began the long process of recuperation after many years of civil strife and political instability. Once again, visitors began to take notice of the beautiful surroundings and temperate climate that San Miguel had to offer. The town's population began to grow once again with the arrival of Spanish immigrants who began buying up land. However, unlike Zeferino Gutiérrez, their impact on the town's appearance would be limited. In 1926, the Mexican government declared the entire town of San Miguel de Allende to be a national historic monument, in order to preserve the town's colonial character.

Birth of an Artists' Colony

The modern, sophisticated city of San Miguel began to take root on a rainy day in 1937 when Felipe Cossío del Pomar—an exiled Peruvian painter and art critic—stepped off the train that had just pulled into town. He was a friend of such notable artists as Diego Rivera and Alfonso Reyes, and had once before been to San Miguel. His ambition was to create a Latin American art school rooted in popular culture and open to all trends of contemporary art. He came to San Miguel to take advantage of the city's reputation as a hospitable place—a place steeped in history that exemplified its colonial past—and one that was isolated from large urban centers as well as the surrounding countryside. He was so committed to seeing his vision to fruition that he was able to garner financial support for his school from Mexico's President, Lázaro Cárdenas. He chose a historic but oddly sacred site as the location of his school: the Convento de Concepción nunnery, located one block from the Jardín Principal—what is today the site of the city's Bellas Artes, or fine arts center. At the time, the building was partially

San Miguel de Allende is a haven for artists of all types.

demolished and occupied by a cavalry regiment of the Mexican army. Cossío offered the position of art director to an American artist and writer named Stirling Dickinson, who had also only recently arrived in San Miguel. Dickinson helped with advertising and promotion as well. He made several trips to various cities in the United States, where he distributed more than ten thousand fliers to universities and cultural centers. The School of Fine Arts of San Miguel de Allende was designed principally to cater to foreign students and wealthy students from Mexico's interior. However, the school also offered popular arts and crafts workshops for local residents of limited means. These workshops focused on preserving various ancestral crafts such as handmade textiles and ceramics that might have otherwise been lost. Thanks to Cossío's full Rolodex, the school hosted many distinguished speakers during its early years, such as Pablo Neruda, Jesús Silva Hérzog, and Diego Rivera. As the school expanded, Cossío acquired an old ranch from a famous bullfighter and turned it into residences for students, professors, and visitors alike. He adapted a huge water tank on the property into an Olympic size pool—complete with showers and dressing rooms—and remodeled the rooms around

The roads of San Miguel de Allende were not constructed with automobiles in mind.

the center patio into eight apartments, modeling them on his Paris studio. He also commissioned a great arch to be built at the lower entrance to the school, atop Calle Santo Domingo. The arch is a perfect replica of a 17th-century baroque arch in Cusco, Peru. However, in 1945 the Peruvian government announced that exiles could return home, prompting Cossío to return to his homeland.

Before he left, Cossío sold his school to a pair of Italian brothers, who promptly made an agreement with the U.S. government to offer special rates to recently returned soldiers who were interested in studying art. Unfortunately, these brothers embezzled the G.I. Bill money and drove the school into ruin. Nevertheless, San Miguel's days as a haven for expatriate veterans were just beginning. In 1948, *Life* magazine published a story about veterans studying art in San Miguel, calling the city a G.I. paradise. The story told of apartments that rented for $10 a month, tended by servants, as well as 65-cent rum and 10-cent packs of cigarettes. Soon, over six thousand American veterans had applied to study art in San Miguel, more than half the number of the city's total population. By this time, the residents of San Miguel had begun to restore the city's colonial architecture and develop other tourist attractions, such as the nearby thermal springs. Some veterans brought their families while others married into local, well-established families. This trend would continue with the later arrival of retirees from north of the border, and names like Brooks, Dickinson, and Hawkins became engrained into the cultural history of San Miguel.

Felipe Cossío del Pomar was once again sent into exile, in 1948. He returned to San Miguel and began a new art school located at the old residences of the de la Canal family, known simply as the Instituto Allende. Again, with the help of Stirling Dickinson as well as that of the retired governor of Guanajuato, Enrique Fernández Martínez, Cossío converted the old de la Canal mansion into an appropriate venue for an art school. In 1951, classes began at the Instituto Allende. Nearly all of the students were from the United States. Today, San Miguel de Allende has a thriving art culture that stands as a testament to the hard work of Cossío and his associates.

In the ensuing years, waves of students arrived annually from north of the border for accredited summer courses and, along the way, many decided to stay. Enterprising locals soon saw the need to teach the newly arrived foreigners the local language, and San Miguel's language schools began to pop up. The Hispano-American

American and Canadian expatriates have long been a part of San Miguel de Allende.

Academy began by organizing classes in Latin American culture as well as symphonic concerts and chamber music. These events were used to restore the Angela Peralta Theater, which was being used as a movie theater at the time. In 1960, after more than 10 years of neglect, the School of Bellas Artes that was begun by Cossío was restored with a government grant, to coincide with the celebration of 150 years of Mexican independence. Little by little, and with very few resources, the school grew to also include instruction in areas such as music. As the city's expatriate movement continued in the counterculture years of the 1960s, it became a popular destination of beat writer Neal Cassady, as well as Ken Kesey, author of *One Flew Over the Cuckoo's Nest*.

Today the atmosphere and ambiance of San Miguel, inarguably favorable for creativity, attracts painters, writers, and musicians from around Mexico and around the world. Moreover, it has all the modern services any urban dweller has come to expect, but with the feel of a small town. Despite an expanding populace and the influx of commercial and tourist development, San Miguel continues to be an artists' colony and a favored destination for expatriates. The artistic and cultural environment that has prospered in San Miguel for nearly 75 years has created a unique society very different from any other in Central Mexico. In fact, what most makes the city unique is the interplay between the traditional Mexican culture, which the city has built upon over the years, and the culture from north of the border, which has been brought here by expatriates from the United States and Canada. In fact, it has become a common saying among American retirees here that one goes to Florida to die and one goes to San Miguel to live.

Transportation

SAN MIGUEL DE ALLENDE and Guanajuato are towns that can only and truly be appreciated on foot. It is only by walking that you experience the ambiance created by open plazas and the colorful houses with carved arched doors. Fortunately, they are both towns that are compact—with hotels, bars, restaurants, and general points of interest situated around a central area, making them ideal for walking. Having stated that, there are also monuments, villages, and other interesting locations that are not within walking distance. You will not have any trouble finding public transportation to take you to these places, though many people like to have the convenience of having their own transportation at hand. Certainly, if you are coming from the southern border region of the United States, the state of Guanajuato is well within driving distance. In fact, this region has become a somewhat popular destination for RV enthusiasts, though I can't imagine trying to navigate an RV through the narrow streets of San Miguel, which were not even constructed with a

Quick tip: Be sure that you are buying a first-class ticket that is "directo." Nondirect trips can have several annoying layovers and bus stations are rarely interesting places to spend time. And a long ride on anything less than first-class can quickly turn into a nightmare.

LEFT: Taxis are generally easy to flag down in the historic centers.

four-door sedan in mind. However you choose to get here, you are sure to find that your best hours will be spent on your feet rather than behind the wheel.

GETTING TO THE AREA

By Air

The biggest challenge of a trip to San Miguel de Allende is probably just getting there. San Miguel de Allende is served by two international airports, though neither one is a convenient choice for anyone accustomed to the convenience of a big city airport nearby. On the bright side, your afternoon coffee in the Jardín Principal will never be disturbed by a jet streaming overhead. The first is Aeropuerto del Bajío (airport code BJX), about halfway between the town of Guanajuato and the city of León, the largest city in the state of Guanajuato. Therefore, if the town of Guanajuato is your primary destination, you will only have a 20-minute cab ride from the airport to your hotel in downtown Guanajuato. However, this airport is about 100 miles away from San Miguel, making it difficult to catch an early morning flight out of town. The airlines operating out of BJX include Continental Airlines, American Airlines, Aeromexico, and Delta Airlines. If you do

Several airlines provide service to the area.

happen to have an early morning flight out of BJX, it might be worth your while to plan on spending your night in the town of Guanajuato. Another option is the recently opened Aeropuerto Internacional de Querétaro (airport code QRO), which lies only 40 miles away outside of the beautiful colonial city of Querétaro. The choice of airlines serving this airport is not as extensive as at BJX, though it is served by Continental Airlines and Aeromexico, with daily nonstop flights from Los Angeles and Houston.

You can arrange to be picked up from the airport through several of the local tour companies. The drivers are bilingual and will take you directly to the doorstep of your hotel—and will pick you up as far away as the Mexico City airport—for as little as $50 per person. This option has the added benefit of providing you at the beginning of your visit with a knowledgeable local tour guide with whom to discuss the ins and outs of this beautiful place.

By Bus

If flying is not the way you like to get around, traveling by bus can be a nice way to tour Mexico and see the countryside in the process. Although Hollywood movies have created an image of Mexican bus travel as that of riding in cramped quarters with several goats and a rooster, many Mexican bus companies provide a more comfortable experience than you'll find in the United States—at extremely reasonable rates. Luxury or first-class buses are modern, with comfortable reclining seats, and are extremely clean. They usually will play an American film, which will more than likely be dubbed in Spanish. Second-class buses are also very clean, but usually lack a bathroom and video monitors. Plus, some second-class buses are notorious for being long rides, because they often stop and pick up passengers anywhere in the countryside.

Both Guanajuato and San Miguel de Allende have modern bus stations fairly close to where you want to be. In San Miguel, it is located on Calle Canal, about 0.5 mile from the center of town. Any local bus marked central heading west on Canal will make a stop at the bus station. Taxis from the bus station to the center of San Miguel are a bargain—20 pesos during the day and usually 25 pesos at night. In Guanajuato, the bus station is located outside of the city core—but a taxi into town will only cost you a few bucks, or you can take the city bus for about a quarter. When in the bus station, always be alert and attentive to your luggage and never leave it unattended. Buses

Mexico has a very modern bus system.

for San Miguel leave from Querétaro about every 20 minutes during the day, and every hour or two in the evening. The trip takes about an hour. **Flecha Amarilla** (473-733-1332; www.flecha-amarilla.com.mx) has nine buses a day with service between San Miguel de Allende and Guanajuato.

If you are crossing the border in Texas, **Transportes del Norte** (473-733-1344) offers first-class bus service to and from Laredo, Texas. If you plan to travel by bus to or from Pacific beach towns such as Acapulco or Zihuatanejo, your best bet is to go through Morelia, Michoacán. You could also connect through Mexico City. However, the logistics of getting in and out of Mexico City will add several hours to your trip.

The first-class bus ride to San Miguel or Guanajuato from Mexico City takes between four and five hours from the city's Terminal Norte. Companies offering this service include **Primera Plus** (473-733-1332; www.primeraplus.com.mx), **ETN** (473-733-1579; www.etn .com.mx), and **Omnibus de Mexico** (473-733-2607; www.odm.com .mx)www.odm.com.mx. These companies offer six daily first-class trips.

You can get to San Miguel de Allende by driving south on Highway 51, which comes from the west through Dolores Hidalgo. However, if you're coming south from Texas, take Highway 85 past Monterrey to the Saltillo Bypass. Here, hop on Highway 57 and continue through Central Mexico into the state of Guanajuato. To get to Guanajuato, pick up Highway 110 out of Dolores Hidalgo or Highway 45 out of León. To get to Guanajuato from Mexico City, there are two routes. The first is to take Highway 57 north past Querétaro to Dolores Hidalgo, then take Highway 110 west to Guanajuato. The faster route, however, is to take Highway 57 north to Querétaro, where you pick up Highway 45D west to Salamanca, then follow Highway 45 north to Silao, and then take Highway 110 east. To get to San Miguel de Allende from Mexico City, take Highway 57 through Querétaro and continue north for about 25 miles. A sign points left to San Miguel de Allende. Exit and continue on that two-lane road for about 20 miles. When you get to San Miguel de Allende, take Salida a Querétaro to the center of town. The quickest way between Guanajuato and San Miguel de Allende is Highway 110 south from Guanajuato. The more scenic route is Highway 110 north out of Guanajuato through Dolores Hidalgo.

Finding parking can be a problem in San Miguel de Allende.

Quick tip: Do not drive at night. The dangers presented by narrow roads, wandering animals, and unprotected cliffs are exacerbated at night. This is especially true of animals, which congregate at the edge of the roadway where the grass grows greenest. One traveler told me that he has successfully navigated Mexican roads at night by sidling up behind trucks as a way of protection against loitering livestock. However, that seems like a lot of trust to put in the hands of the trucker in front of you. The best advice is to find a place to get some rest, and get going again in the morning when it's safe.

Long distance driving in Mexico is a challenging pursuit, even for drivers who have plenty of experience driving long distances north of the border. Even the most modern Mexican highways are not engineered with the same eye toward safety that you find in the United States. Driving in larger Mexican cities can be an intimidating undertaking, with other drivers prying their way into the smallest opening in traffic and putting the onus on you to avoid a collision—as well as treating stop signs and traffic lights as mere suggestions instead of requirements. With regards to Mexico's open roads, these circumstances cease and the greatest danger is quite the opposite of intimidating traffic; here the biggest danger is complacency. One of the most common dangers is the livestock that commonly wander onto the road. This is generally not a problem if you are minding your speed. However, you do *not* want to come careening through a mountain pass to find a herd of cattle sitting on the road ahead of you. Another slightly related problem is the lack of guardrails that exist on the roads, even where they wind along steep cliffs. Getting to Guanajuato by car from the U.S. border requires driving highways that weave through the mountains of Northern and Central Mexico. As you drive through areas such as these, it will become abundantly clear that the road was not engineered with the kind of safety standards that are common north of the border. Add to this the frequent potholes and the steep or nonexistent shoulder.

If I still haven't talked you out of it, taking Mexican toll roads from Nuevo Laredo to Guanajuato or San Miguel de Allende can add up to around $70 in toll fees. These roads are marked as *cuota* on road signs and maps. There are free highways that will take you to the area (marked as *libre*), but these roads are generally two-lane highways and not well maintained. This means stretches that are even more treacherous than normal, and you are guaranteed to encounter slow-moving trucks that will crawl along for miles before pulling to the shoulder or giving you the opportunity to pass safely.

Speed limits are posted in kilometers. This can be a bit confusing if your speedometer does not include kilometers. However, since 60 miles per hour is roughly equal to 100 kilometers per hour, if you multiply the posted speed limit by 6 and drop the last zero, that will give you a rough estimation of the allowed speed in miles per hour.

Keep in mind that while it can be a convenience to have your own car to travel between towns and other destinations, a car can easily turn into a hindrance here as well. Both San Miguel de Allende and (especially) Guanajuato are notoriously difficult places to find parking. Unless your hotel has private parking, you could have a tough time finding a place to leave your car. Remember that both Guanajuato and San Miguel are places where you can get from place to place just fine on foot. When driving, be sure to purchase Mexican insurance before crossing over into Mexico, since most U.S. auto insurance does not cover driving in Mexico. Mexican drivers tend to be aggressive, not to mention the fact that stop signs and traffic lights tend to be treated as mere suggestions rather than hard-and-fast rules.

Insurance

Under Mexican law, in the event of an accident motorists are required to have sufficient currency to cover damages, or insurance from a Mexican company. Non-Mexican insurance does not fulfill this responsibility. If you are involved in an automobile accident, you are basically considered guilty until proven innocent. You will be detained until the local authorities determine who is at fault. If this happens, it is a good idea to contact your nearest consulate immediately. You will be required to demonstrate financial responsibility. Financial responsibility is defined as being in possession of an inexpensive Mexican insurance policy or $5,000 to $10,000 in cash. Therefore, it is not a good idea to drive in Mexico without Mexican liability insurance. If you are renting a car, you will pay for this insurance through the rental company. However, if you are driving your own vehicle into Mexico, you'll need to purchase insurance on your own. This insurance is relatively inexpensive, and it comes with peace of mind.

Plenty of companies offer this insurance at all major U.S.–Mexico border crossings and on the Internet. **Adventure Mexican Insurance** (1-800-485-4075; www.mexadventure.com) has been in business for many years and can provide you with an instant quote. Likewise, **Instant Mexico Auto Insurance** (1-800-345-4701; www.instant-mex -auto-insur.com) has been in business since 1973 and can provide you with a policy over the Internet. **Mexpro Mexican Auto Insurance** (1-888-467-4639; www.mexpro.com) is an insurance broker that will offer you options from many different companies.

Military Stops

If you travel by road in Mexico, you will soon experience being stopped at a military checkpoint. For the average American who is not used to such things, this can be a jarring experience. After all, you just came down here to have a good time, right? Just keep in mind that everybody goes through this, and it isn't really a big deal. Despite what you may have heard about corrupt cops demanding payola, Mexico's economy depends on the influx of tourist dollars. It would not be in their interest to have the authorities shaking down every tourist who comes along. As long as you've done nothing wrong, you have nothing to worry about.

These stops are actually largely the result of Mexico attempting to satisfy their allies from north of the border that they are doing everything in their power to stop the flow of drugs northward. Keep in mind that these young soldiers are just doing their job. Many of them come from the poorer parts of Mexico, and they are occasionally even illiterate— meaning that your political opinions about unwarranted searches could hardly have less significance to them. Therefore, it is best just to cooperate so you can be on your way.

Generally, you will be stopped for only a few minutes. The soldiers will likely ask to see your identification and to look in

> **Did you know?**
>
> Guns are illegal in Mexico. There have been cases of Americans unwittingly crossing the border into Mexico while in possession of firearms that are perfectly legal in the United States—only to find themselves locked up for months and even years in a Mexican prison. *Do not take firearms into Mexico with you.*

your trunk. It is always a nice gesture to offer them a cold soda on a hot day. Assuming that you are not carrying any drugs, guns, or other illegal paraphernalia, you will soon be on your way.

Stopping for Gas

Petroleos Mexicanos—or PEMEX—is Mexico's state-owned national-ized petroleum company. Its midgrade gasoline, Magna Sin, is rated at 87 octane and should be fine for cars that run on unleaded regular in the United States. Mexican Premium is rated at 92 octane.

Though PEMEX stations are not as abundant as gas stations north of the border, you will find them in all major stops on your itin-erary. They are generally open 24 hours a day, and they do not take credit cards; pesos or dollars only. The upside to this is that PEMEX stations make a great place to break large bills since the attendants carry a lot of cash. Speaking of the attendants, they will pump your gas and clean your windshield if you need it. It is customary to tip them about 10 pesos, less than $1.

Customs and Immigration

Technically speaking, customs and immigration can be a real pain. You can mitigate some of this inconvenience by either driving in, or crossing the border and flying out of Ciudad Juárez, Tijuana, or some other Mexican airport. Crossing the U.S.–Mexico border on foot or by car is much less of a hassle than making your way through airport security these days. Furthermore, while a passport is required to fly into the United States from Mexico, citizens of the United States and Canada ages 19 or older need only a government-issued photo ID (such as a driver's license) along with proof of citizenship (such as a birth certificate or naturalization certificate) in order to enter or depart the United States by land or sea. Children ages 18 and younger need proof of citizenship, such as a birth certificate. Eventu-ally, passports will be required even to cross the border on foot. For specific details of current passport rules, check out the Depart-ment of Homeland Security Web site (www.dhs.gov/xtrvlsec/crossing borders/whtibasics.shtm).

A tourist card is an official Mexican document declaring that you have stated that the purpose of your visit to Mexico is tourism and that your visit will last no more than 180 days. This document costs $20 and anyone staying in Mexico for more than 72 hours and travel-ing beyond the border zone (about 70 miles south) needs to have a tourist card. If you are driving into Mexico, you can get this document at the immigration station just across the border. If you are flying out of a Mexican airport, such as Ciudad Juárez, you will get this document as you pass into the boarding area of the airport. And if you are flying into Mexico from another country (such as Canada or the United States), the cost of this document is included in the price of your airfare and you will receive it, along with instructions on filling it out, while on the plane. Once you arrive, customs and immigration will stamp it, indicating that you are in the country legally.

> **Quick tip:** If you don't already have a passport, apply immediately. Even if you're not sure you're going to need it, it's best to have it anyway. And getting one via a rush application can be expensive.

Traveling with Kids

These historic towns in Central Mexico can be great places to take a break from your day-to-day responsibilities. On the other hand, you will probably find yourself constantly thinking it would have been great to bring the kids. If you do decide to take the kids along, there are extra hoops you will have to jump through. First, new passport

Guanajuato's many plazas are a great place for kids to play.

Bringing your Pet to Mexico

Mexico allows dogs and cats into the country as long as the owner has a notarized letter from a veterinarian stating that the animal is in good health and has the proper vaccinations. However, if you're driving, it's unlikely that this will be an issue. Keep in mind that certain risks are to be considered before bringing an animal down to Mexico. Very few hotels allow pets, and those that do generally charge extra. (Be sure to check ahead when making reservations.) However, the biggest danger with regard to pets is that Mexican towns have a problem with stray animals. There is always an outside chance that your animal could contract a disease from one of these animals or that some mishap may occur.

requirements for U.S. citizens returning from abroad also apply to children. Getting a passport for a child under the age of 14 requires filling out additional documents as well as having both parents' consent to their child being taken out of the country. That said, it is no longer necessary for single parents or unaccompanied minors traveling in Mexico to have notarized documentation authorizing travel as long as each child has a valid passport and tourist card.

Car Rental

Though it is quite likely that you will discover that a car is unnecessary and even inconvenient in San Miguel de Allende and Guanajuato, there is always the chance that you will be in a situation where you need one. In Guanajuato, the León airport is generally the best place to rent a car. Because San Miguel de Allende has no airport, none of the big companies that you are familiar with operate there. There are, however, a couple smaller outfits that rent cars as well as ATVs and motorcycles. Of course, you could always rent your car at either the León or Querétaro airports.

Taxis

Taxis are a fairly inexpensive option for getting around. As with most taxi places in Mexico, taxis here generally charge a flat rate for transportation within certain zones. If you are unsure what the rate should

Stopping for ice cream in San Miguel de Allende. Maria Miller Kisska

Car Rental Companys

GUANAJUATO

Alamo Car Rental

472-748-2069

www.alamo.com

Carretera Silao-León Km 5.5

León International Airport

Open: Daily 6 AM–midnight

Avis Rent a Car

472-748-2054

www.avis.com.mx

Carretera Silao-León Km 6.5

León International Airport

Open: Daily 6 AM–11:30 PM

Hertz Car Rental

472-748-2015

www.hertz.com.mx

Carretera Silao-León Km 5.5

León International Airport

Open 24 hours

SAN MIGUEL DE ALLENDE

Hola Rent a Car

415-152-0198

www.holarentacar.com.mx

Plaza Principal #2

Open: Mon.–Sat. 9 AM–2:30 PM; Sun. 4:30 PM–7 PM

Moto Rent

415-152-0023

Salida a Celaya Km 1 #97

Open: Daily 9 AM–8 PM

Taxi Companys

GUANAJUATO

Central de Radio	473-732-9394
Linea Dorado	473-734-1026
Radio Taxi Group	473-732-6649

SAN MIGUEL DE ALLENDE

Radio Taxi	415-152-4501
Sitio Allende	415-152-0192
Taxi Express	415-152-4475
Tel-Taxi	415-152-3134

be, be sure to ask the front desk clerk at your hotel. In general, however, the daytime fare within town is a little bit more than $1; after 9 PM, the cost goes up to around $2. Keep in mind that taxi drivers will charge you double this price if you call them to pick you up. This covers the trip to come and get you as well as the trip to drop you off at your destination. Taxis are generally plentiful in San Miguel and Guanajuato and you usually won't have any trouble finding one to wave down.

Getting Around Guanajuato

When packing for your trip to Guanajuato, a comfortable pair of walking shoes should be the first thing you stuff into your bag. When you are here, you will be doing a lot of walking. The Guanajuato that you have come to see is a compact old city located in a bowl-shaped valley, perhaps 1 mile across and a few miles long. Within this small area are a myriad of beautiful buildings, gorgeous vistas, and café-lined plazas. In the very heart of it—from east of Jardín de la Unión west to the tip of Plaza de La Paz, and for a city block on either side—there are no streets open to traffic. Spreading out from there, there are only narrow one-way cobblestone streets where driving is at a snail's pace even when there is no traffic.

Quick tip: Remember to always ask the price of the ride before getting in the car—or better yet, know the going rate and state that price to the driver in the form of a question. Even the most experienced travelers have been hit by the "gringo tax" every now and then. If the driver quotes you a price that seems too high, don't be afraid to say, "No gracias," and find another taxi.

The sidewalks of Guanajuato can be narrow, steep, and elevated.

The town is actually served by an intricate series of underground roads that were originally constructed as a flood prevention system. Before they were built, the town would occasionally suffer terrible floods when rainwater would pour into the narrow valley where the city is located. In 1883, the construction on the first tunnel got off to a fitful start. However, after a major flood in 1905, city elders decided to commit themselves to the tunnel and to open other routes as well, drawing upon the city's mining resources to complete the job. In 1908, the Tunel de la Cuajín was completed with great fanfare. However, as the 20th century progressed, it became increasingly clear that the town's streets, designed for the horse and carriage, would not suffice with modern modes of transportation. Unwilling to tear up their historic city in order to build wider roads, Guanajuato's residents decided to modify the underground flood tunnels to accommodate traffic. By this time, the town's engineers had built a series of dams surrounding the city, redirecting flood-prone rivers into underground caverns. The tunnels were then lit and paved with cobblestones and widened just enough for automobile traffic. Today, there are about 5 miles of underground roads that carry the majority of cars driving through the town center. These tunnels have also allowed the city to expand outside of the small valley, though there is little of interest outside of this compact center.

If you are driving, be sure to study road maps of the city and figure out exactly how to get where you're going before you set out for the first time. The tunnels are completely confusing if you're not familiar with them and, since they are all one-way, you could end up on a long and frustrating drive if you take the wrong tunnel.

In the center of town, it is perfectly safe to walk inside these tunnels. There is a pedestrian entrance on the west side of Jardín de la

The tunnels that now connect Guanajuato were originally for flood prevention.

Unión next to the Templo San Diego, several along Calle Alonzo, and one on Calle Positos near the Mesón del los Poetas hotel. Aside from the tunnels, the streets and alleyways of Guanajuato can seem like a convoluted maze. As such, you may want to take an afternoon to get lost in these streets just to see where they take you. Duck into one of the steep alleys—possibly as narrow as a few feet—and you will invariably come out the other side to discover a beautiful plaza or an interesting street lined with shops and museums. To be sure, walks around Guanajuato range from the brisk to the strenuous. While the majority of the town's sites are within easy walking distance, there are a few that are farther off—including

The pavestones that line the streets and sidewalks are extremely slippery when wet.

El Pípila monument and Museo de las Momias. For these, you may consider taking the city bus or even springing for a taxi.

Getting Around
San Miguel de Allende

The vast majority of San Miguel's attractions are within walking distance of the center of town. That said, you will also find that it is common to get around town on ATVs—which might be a good option for anyone disinclined to walking. Although San Miguel's topography is nowhere near as hilly as Guanajuato's, it is situated on a mountainside. The streets are flatter on the north side of the city,

Quick tip: If you're visiting during the rainy season, be extra careful when walking along wet streets. The streets of San Miguel and Guanajuato have dangerous grades to begin with. The cobblestones, worn smooth by decades and perhaps centuries of use, are very slick after it rains.

making for relatively easy walking. On the south side, where wealthy neighborhoods are built around Parque Benito Juárez, the streets are much steeper—some streets here can have inclines of as much as 20 degrees. Getting around can be a workout; just keep in mind that it's good for you. Also, in addition to being beautiful, cobblestone streets are hard on the feet. Make sure you have a good pair of comfortable shoes. Luckily, if you forget them, this region is known for its shoes and buying a pair won't be a problem. And make sure to pay attention to where you are walking at all times. Many of the sidewalks are very old and not in the best shape. Curbs are not made to the same specifications in Mexico, and can be several feet above the street in places. If you trip on an upturned pavestone in just the right spot, your vacation can take a bad turn very quickly.

If you have your own car, you might consider leaving it in a parking lot on the outskirts of the city. It's entirely unnecessary for getting around town and road conditions can be murder on your suspension. Keep in mind that driving in San Miguel can be a frustrating experience. The influx of well-to-do foreigners has also meant an influx of American automobiles on roads that were never meant to support them. Even some two-way streets are far too narrow to realistically allow such traffic flows. In fact, in some parts of the city burros are still used to deliver goods because they can do it much more efficiently than any truck. Parking is also famously scarce. A good alternative to driving your own car is to take one of the city's taxis, which are extremely inexpensive and reliable. Additionally, San Miguel has its own pleasant and reliable bus system that serves the entire town, including out-of-the-way areas like the Gigante supermarket or the bus depot.

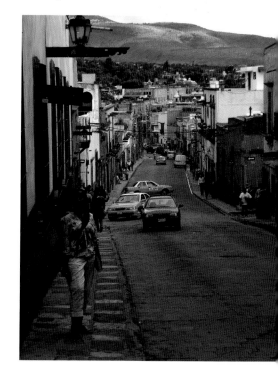

Walking is the best way to get around San Miguel de Allende.

1

San Miguel de Allende

THE REMAINS OF THE 18TH CENTURY alone would warrant a visit. However, this rich colonial history with matching architecture is not what most makes Guanajuato and San Miguel de Allende unique and inviting. Mexico is full of picturesque colonial towns that have moseyed into the 21st century surrounded by remnants of a more glorious past. What makes these two towns worth your while is the vibrant and creative life that is taking place in them today.

This vibrancy comes from distinct and even surprising sources. It is a common complaint about San Miguel that the culture here has somehow been watered down by the five thousand or so American and Canadian expatriates that now call this city home. First of all, it's not as if the city has really been overrun by foreigners. Expats are still a small minority of San Miguel de Allende's population. Secondly, it is not as though the last 60 years have seen this city descended upon by a multitude of retired accountants (not that I have anything against accountants, of course). By and large, these expatriates have been highly creative, daring people who have come to reinvent themselves by doing what they've always wanted to do. In the process, they have reinvented San Miguel de Allende, making it an active artists' colony where just about anything seems possible. No, the town is not as traditional as it might otherwise be—but hey, if Spanish is not your strong suit, this may be the easiest town in Central Mexico for you to get along in.

LEFT: The interior of Parroquia de San Miguel.

The Jardín Allende is the heart of San Miguel.

Jardín Allende at the intersection of Cuna de Allende and Principal de Correo is located at the cultural and historical heart of San Miguel de Allende. It is a lovely city square with manicured gardens of rose bushes and laurels, all surrounded by beautiful buildings and archways from the colonial era. The center of the plaza is a verdant garden known as Jardín Allende. Its lawns are crisscrossed by cobblestone paths on the circumference that also cut through the center. You will find a shaded gazebo here, and the perimeter of the square is lined by sculpted trees. On

Quick tip: When conversing in English with locals, try to speak in grammatically correct sentences and avoid using slang. However, don't speak unnecessarily slowly or in disjointed sentences. This can understandably come across as insulting.

the north side of the square an 18th-century building houses the municipal government, flanked by several small businesses and restaurants. On the south side, a line of park benches faces the city's most famous church, the Parroquia de San Miguel. This is a great place to sit under the shade of the trees and relax for a half hour or so. Here you're sure to find plenty of American retirees lounging away the afternoon, and artists with their easels and brushes out. On Saturday evenings, the traditional promenade of young people circles the square to the sounds of mariachis and other live musicians. Boys walk the perimeter of the Jardín Allende in one direction and the girls circle in the other direction, while parents watch from the park benches.

Pick Your Spot

Best places to stay in San Miguel de Allende, and what you'll find nearby . . .

ON AND OFF JARDÍN ALLENDE

Posada de San Francisco (415-152-7213; www.posadadesan francisco.com) is located right on the city's central plaza, offering guests the ability to step out the front door and right into the middle of things. It features 46 rooms and suites decorated in a simple but comfortable Mexican style. The walls are not overburdened with art, but there's something about it that tells you you're in Mexico. Standard rooms are fairly small and are furnished with a queen-sized

Residents enjoying a beautiful day in San Miguel.

The Jardín Allende bustles with life.

bed. Suites are furnished with two queen-sized beds and have a living room area. However, the main attraction here is the location and the hotel itself. There is bar and food service in the interior courtyard and the restaurant has large arches that open onto the street, making it a great place for people watching.

A block north of Jardín Allende, Casa Linda (415-154-4007; www.hotelcasalinda.com) combines the charm of a rustic colonial with modern amenities. There are 10 suites appointed with original Mexican art and *artesenia* as well as private fireplaces and kitchenettes. Each room is individually decorated with handmade furniture and colorful additions such as hand-stitched pillows and colorfully woven placemats. These rooms are relatively spacious and beautifully decorated with hardwood or tiled floors and elegant antique furnishings. After a long day of trudging up and down San Miguel's cobblestone streets, you'll be happy to take advantage of the in-room spa service that is available. If you are not a guest of the hotel, you can always pay a visit to the on-site day spa that is open to the public by appointment. The hotel's restaurant, Nirvana, serves breakfast, lunch, and dinner daily from 8:30 AM to 10 PM. This is a great place to sit on the patio and take in the gorgeous colonial surroundings on a warm day. Additionally, the hotel offers room service from several of the nearby restaurants—for weary travelers or those just wanting a romantic evening alone.

El Alcázar Hotel (415-152-0354; www.elalcazarcasahotel.com.mx), a beautifully rustic establishment, has the kind of stone architecture you come to San Miguel to see. Located just one block south of Jardín Allende, this boutique hotel offers six rooms within quick walking distance of shops, restaurants, and other important points on your itinerary. Breakfast is included with each night's stay. The relatively spacious rooms feature bathrooms decked out in colorful Mexican tile. The rooms are clean and appointed in brightly colored Mexican blankets and traditional folk art. They are also surprisingly quiet, considering the hotel's central location. The hotel's rooftop terrace offers an ideal place to relax with a drink and watch dusk fall over the city. The coffee shop is open from 7 AM to 10 PM.

Enjoying breakfast at the Posada de San Francisco.

Quick tip: If you are visiting during the peak tourist season or during one of the region's many festivals, consider finding a hotel that is a few blocks away from the action. Noisy crowds jam up the entrances of the plaza hotels, sometimes actually making it harder to get to your room than if it was located on a nearby back street. What's worse is that these crowds create quite a ruckus. If your room has a window that opens onto the street, it will catch all that noise, making your room sound like a frat party. And even if you plan on being part of the late-night party, it's always good to have a nice quiet place to relax just in case. Therefore, what you give up in convenience you will get back several times over in a good night's sleep.

Right across the street, **Casa Rosada** (415-152-8123; www .casarosadahotel.com) is located in an 18th-century residence. Rooms are sparsely decorated with neutral colors and a combination of Mexican, Hindu, and Moroccan art. Casa Rosada offers seven standard rooms, three junior suites, and three master suites. Master suites include a living room and a private terrace, and junior suites have a balcony or a small terrace. The standard rooms are fairly roomy, and are certainly comfortable and attractive. The rooms are simply and tastefully appointed and include cable TV and wireless Internet access. Some rooms also have air-conditioning, which can be a big plus in the summertime. Standard room rates are on the high side of moderate, while master suites are quite a bit more expensive. The on-site Xipal restaurant offers elegant Mexican cuisine and is open daily from 7 PM to 10 PM.

Also on this block, **Posada Carmina** (415-152-0458; www .posadacarmina.com) is located in another 18th-century colonial villa. It offers 24 elegantly appointed rooms furnished with either one king-sized bed or two doubles. Rooms are not colorful, but instead put an emphasis on moderation, with only a touch of Mexican tile here and there. The rooms are built around an attractive arch-filled cobblestone courtyard, a perfect place for relaxing and planning the day. The restaurant is a remodeled stable and has an attractive fireplace, wrought-iron windows,

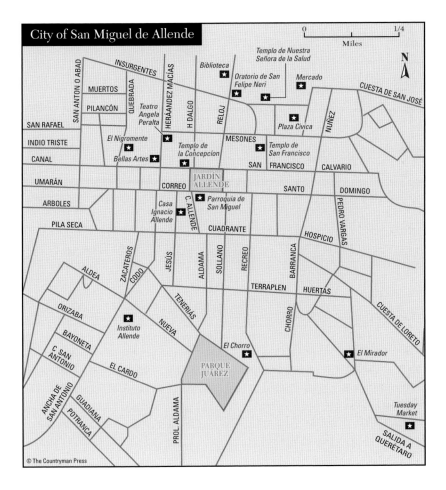

and large stone arch that almost take you back to the colonial days of the 18th century. It offers indoor and courtyard seating. There is wireless Internet access in this area of the hotel. This restaurant offers a traditional daily *comida* (meal of the day). It is open daily from 7:30 AM to 11 PM. Don't miss the two-for-one happy hour Monday through Friday from 5 PM to 8 PM.

Half a block down the street, the **Posada Corazón** (415-152-0182; www.posada corazon.com.mx) features six rooms diversely decorated that open onto a central garden courtyard. The rooms are simple but elegant, with touches like carved marble headboards and handmade sitting chairs. One suite features a private patio pool. The main house itself is decorated with a nice blend of rustic and modern appointments such as exposed stone walls and a small library. There is also a comfortable living room containing a small library, and a stone patio which is a nice place for just relaxing. The property is equipped with wireless Internet access and private parking. An organic breakfast is included with each night's stay. Additionally, private massages and gourmet coffee drinks are also available.

Around the corner, the **Oasis** (415-154-9850; www.oasis sanmiguel.com), a Moroccan-themed bed and breakfast hotel, is located in a converted 17th-century villa with four elegantly appointed suites. The Bedouin and Berber Suites feature a king-sized bed, extra large shower, and French doors that open onto a private wall fountain and pond. The Sahara Suite features a king-sized four-poster bed and shuttered windows with a nice view of San Miguel. The Nomad Suite features a king-sized four-poster bed and a hand-carved Mudejar daybed. The room also has a Moroccan-style bath with double vanities, and a water wall that stretches the length of the suite. As with all the suites, a gourmet breakfast is provided with each night's stay. Each suite has a private fireplace, wireless Internet, and flat screen TV.

Additionally, the property has a rooftop terrace with a 360-degree view of the city.

Three blocks west of the Jardín Allende on Calle Canal, **Posada de las Monjas** (415-152-0171; www.posadalasmonjas .com) is a 64-room hotel that resembles a small castle. Despite the fact that it shows its age, it provides clean accommodations. Guests are offered laundry service for a nominal fee. The reception area has a nice fireplace and is an inviting place to relax and have a conversation. The rooms are not fancy or particularly spacious. However, the beds are surprisingly soft and comfortable. Plus, if you can get a room on the top floor, your room will not only be quiet but you will have a nice view of the city as well. Be warned, however, there is no elevator and it can be quite a workout. If you're traveling on a budget, you could do much worse. Triple occupancy rooms are available.

NORTH OF JARDÍN ALLENDE

Several blocks north of Jardín Allende, at Calle Mesones and Calle Colegio, you will find **Plaza Civica**. This square was constructed in honor of Don Ignacio Allende. In the center of the square is an equestrian

The Plaza Civica was constructed to honor Don Ignacio Allende.

statue of Allende astride his horse, with his saber heroically held aloft in his right hand. This square is bordered by the building that was the prestigious school of San Francisco de Sales in the 18th century, as well as the Iglesia de Nuestra Señora de la Salud (Church of Our Lady of Health). It is a quiet place with few vendors or shops. If you are traveling with small children, this would be a good place to bring them to run around or bounce a ball if you have some time to kill.

Between Plaza Civica and Jardín Allende, Casa Calderoni (415-154-6005; www.casacalderoni.com) features nine rooms, each one dedicated to and named after a different artist. The rooms are not the largest in town but they are comfortably appointed and tastefully decorated in an elegant colonial or southwestern style with tiled bathrooms, handmade tile floors, solid wood furniture, and wrought-iron bed frames. The higher-end suites are much roomier and feature sofa beds. This hotel also features a rooftop terrace with an outstanding view of the city. Pets and children under 14 are not allowed. The

A Few Words About Bathrooms and Toilet Paper

One of the less delicate issues that you will quickly face when you are traveling in Mexico, particularly in less tourist-centered areas, is the difference in bathroom etiquette. Toilet paper tends to clog most Mexican plumbing and septic systems to the point where it sometimes even requires digging up the pipes to clear them. Therefore, it is necessary to deposit used paper into the wastebasket that is invariably placed next to the toilet. Many moderate and expensive hotels understand that this is more than a minor culture shock to their American guests and have gone through the trouble of equipping rooms with plumbing that can handle toilet paper. However, you shouldn't assume this is the case unless there is a sign posted in the bathroom directing you to flush toilet paper. Still, part of the draw of San Miguel and Guanajuato is the architecture, and many of these old buildings simply have not been brought up to the standards that you are used to. Quite often, there will be a sign explicitly asking you *not* to flush your used toilet paper. Also, women should never flush feminine products. You may find this unpleasant but it's better than dealing with a stopped-up toilet in your room.

There are other differences that you are likely to run into when

standard room and junior suite rates are inexpensive and full suite rates are not much more.

Located just above the *Mercado de Artesenias*, **Casa de la Cuesta** (415-154-4324; www .casadelacuesta.com) is an elegant B&B that offers six individually appointed rooms with private fireplaces and access to a terrace that overlooks San Miguel and the nearby mountains. They open onto a central patio with a tiled stone fountain, providing the atmosphere of an authentic Mexican villa.

Throughout the property are numerous Mexican-style arched doorways, and the walls are covered with traditional art. Each room is furnished with one king-sized bed that can be converted to two singles. The floors are beautifully tiled and decorated in a colonial style. The common dining room is tiled, with an attractive fireplace and a high beamed ceiling, and decorated in a way that makes you feel right at home (though children under 16 are not allowed). A full Mexican you are out and about and discover that you need to use the public restroom. First of all, janitorial work is largely considered "women's work" in Central Mexico. Therefore, it is always possible that men may be surprised by an elderly female janitor entering the restroom while they are taking care of their business. If this happens, do your best to maintain a blasé attitude, remembering that you're not doing anything she hasn't dealt with before. You will likely find well-stocked facilities in higher-end establishments that cater to tourists. However, you cannot always count on this. More often, public restrooms will cost a few pesos and an attendant will hand you a few squares of toilet paper when you enter. There are still other places where you will find no toilet paper at all, and perhaps even the toilet seats will be missing. It's best to be well prepared, especially if you are traveling with children—who seem to have the habit of having to go at the worst possible times. Be sure to pack a roll of toilet paper or—even better—a travel pack of baby wipes before you leave your hotel for the day. It is also a very good idea to pack a small bottle of disinfectant lotion, which you can pick up at any drugstore or pharmacy. This will go a long way toward making sure you don't pick up any of those nasty digestion problems that Mexico is so famous for.

breakfast is complimentary with every night's stay.

SOUTH OF JARDÍN ALLENDE

Due south of Jardín Allende, at Calle Hermanos Aldama and Calle Diezmo, Parque Benito Juárez is a large, well-kept park (though there is a bit of a graffiti problem). It is located three blocks south of Jardín Allende along Calle Hermanos Aldama. There is a playground here with an old-style metal border. However, it is often filled with healthy kids having a good time. There are also picnic tables and charcoal grills here, as well as basketball courts that tend to fill up when school lets out. La Mansión del Bosque (415-152-0277; www.mansiondelbosque .com) is a warm and inviting B&B that is located off Parque Juárez, three blocks from the city center. It offers 23 rooms, each with its own private fireplace and access to semiprivate terraces. They are comfortably appointed in a rustic Mexican

Enjoying a game of basketball in Parque Benito Juárez

style that quickly makes you feel at home. Guests are welcome to bring along small pets; however, be sure to mention this when you make your reservations. The owner, a published cookbook author, personally supervises the kitchen—designing a different menu from fresh local ingredients every day. After dinner, head to the outdoor patio and enjoy a drink from the hotel bar. It's a perfect way to end a long day of traveling.

Just a few blocks south of Jardín Allende, there are several hotels and B&Bs that take advantage of the city's colonial architecture to offer uniquely Mexican experiences. **Casa Diana** (415-152-0885; www.casa -diana.com) is a B&B boutique hotel that offers three rooms in a restored colonial house just 2.5 blocks from the Principal. It was restored by surrealist artist Pedro Friedeberg. The first floor of the house is a gallery featuring work of several artists, while the second floor houses the guest rooms—though the entire house is uniquely decorated. For example, you will find the original work of Friedeberg throughout the house. This sitting area is adorned with a lion-face chimney and the second-floor terrace has a miniature Indian temple. A gourmet breakfast is included with the price of your room. Breakfast is served either on the second-floor terrace or in the gallery area.

Casa de Sierra Nevada Hotel (415-152-7040; www.casa desierranevada.com) is actually a collection of four houses within several blocks of one another offering 32 rooms and suites in all. Because of the hotel's unique circumstances, no two rooms are alike—though they are all decorated with richly colored art and antiques as well as tiled bathrooms and Mexican furniture. Many have fireplaces, while others have terraces opening onto the streets of San Miguel. Additionally, this hotel functions as a cooking school, offering classes in gourmet Mexican cooking. If you are planning a trip to San Miguel for a wedding or other event, this hotel has several venues on-site. Besides the facilities available in the hotel, the Casa de Sierra Nevada offers three event spaces for meetings, presentations, receptions, and banquets. No guests under the age of 16 are allowed.

Just down the street, Hacienda de las Flores (415-152-1808; www.haciendadelas flores.com) offers 17 brightly appointed rooms which are arranged in a variety of accommodation configurations. There are special rates available for longer stays, and children under

A young couple strolls through Parque Juárez.

12 stay for free. The hotel grounds are ideal for large groups as well as special events, such as weddings or reunions. The property has several nicely landscaped gardens and a good-sized patio swimming pool. There is also a garden bar and a rooftop Jacuzzi. The restaurant serves up a menu of Mexican favorites. Breakfast is served daily from 8 AM to noon, and lunch and larger parties by appointment.

If you're looking for elegant charm, you won't go wrong with **Dos Casas** (415-152-4958; www .livingdoscasas.com). This is a beautifully appointed boutique hotel located just three blocks from the town's main plaza. It is decorated with an interesting blend of modern and colonial decors. It offers six stylish suites with dark-stained high-beamed ceilings and handmade tile bathrooms. They are decorated in cool neutral colors and exposed-stone walls. Several have canopy beds for that added romantic touch. The property also has a rooftop terrace with full bar and light snacks, open daily from noon to 8 PM. There is an elegant wine bar on the property that is open Tuesday through Sunday from 1 PM to 10 PM. Guests are offered walking and bicycle tours of the city, as well as in-room spa services and

cooking classes. Private parties are also available.

Casa de Líza (415-152-0352; www.casaliza.com) is located in a 17th-century colonial estate. Its American owner purchased the estate in the 1980s and set about creating a distinctive guest house designed to provide a unique experience. The hotel features eight unique accommodation options ranging from luxury suites to casitas (small houses complete with full kitchens). You will be greeted with fresh flowers grown in the hotel's private greenhouse. Rooms boast features such as fireplaces, elegantly carved French doors, and Jacuzzi bathtubs. Some rooms have king-sized beds while others have two twins that can be pushed together to create one queen-sized bed. A gourmet breakfast of eggs, cereals, and seasonal fresh fruit is provided when and where you want, even if that happens to be in bed. Appetizers are also served around the heated pool in the late afternoon. All rooms have cable TV and Internet access. Additional on-site salon services such as manicure/pedicure, hair styling, and massage therapy are also available by appointment. Suite rates are moderate while casitas are a bit more expensive.

One of San Miguel's more

interesting hotels is located three (long) blocks southwest of the main square, just across the street from the Arte School Instituto Allende. Pablo Suites (415-152-2916; www.pablosuites.com) takes its name from the owner; however, there are a couple dozen photos of other famous Pablos (or Pauls) throughout the hotel—including Newman, Neruda, and (of course) Picasso. There are four suites, each one named after a particular Pablo. They are spacious and elegantly appointed in a modern style with either one king-sized bed or two double beds and a living room area. A continental breakfast is provided with each night's stay. The rates here are inexpensive, but it certainly doesn't seem like a budget hotel.

Roughly translated as "whisper," Susurro (415-152-1065; www.susurro.com.mx) earns its name with quiet elegance. Located just three blocks off Jardín Allende, this B&B hotel is actually an 18th-century colonial mansion with lush gardens, tiled patios, and a pool. The property was purchased in 2001 by its American expatriate owner, and restored to its current elegant condition. It retains a colonial feel with beamed ceilings and arched doorways. A gourmet breakfast is included with each

night's stay, served either in the dining room, the garden courtyard, or on your private terrace. With only four suites, this hotel provides very intimate accommodations. Rooms feature private tiled bathrooms; hand-carved fireplaces; and king-, queen-, or two twin-sized beds.

Located in a two-story mansion, Villa Mirasol Hotel (415-152-8057; www.villamirasolhotel.com) offers 10 suites that are fairly spacious and decorated in a simple manner that draws on natural light, making you feel right at home. Rooms are furnished with either king-, queen-, or two twin-sized beds and feature private patio areas. All in all, this is a very comfortable hotel. Breakfast is included with each night's stay and there is a complimentary teatime service between 5 PM and 6 PM. Just in case you want to shake up your itinerary, guests of the hotel also receive access to the local country club for swimming, tennis, and golf.

AROUND TOWN

One of San Miguel's longest continuously running hotels, the Antigua Villa Santa Mónica (415-152-0427; www.antiguavillasantamonica.com) is located in an 18th-century hacienda originally owned by a Spanish silver baron. It opened its doors as a hotel in 1940 and continues to offer luxury service and colonial charm. Its 14 rooms feature handmade tile and wood-beamed ceilings, and they are furnished with romantic wrought-iron four-poster beds shrouded with linens. They also feature brightly colored Mexican earthenware called *talavera* and regional rugs, creating a distinctly Mexican ambiance. The on-site restaurant is open from Tuesday through Sunday and features an extensive menu and wine list. Breakfast is served from 7:30 AM to noon and lunch from 1 PM to 5:30 PM. This is a great place for a romantic get-away but not for a family vacation. Children under eight are not allowed.

Located a brisk uphill walk from the city center, La Puertecita Boutique Hotel (415-152-5011; www.lapuertecita .com) offers luxury accommodations with a colonial feel. The grounds of the hotel are lush and well manicured, with crawling vines next to close-cropped hedges. Spa service is offered poolside, with facials and body massages. The hotel also has an elegant restaurant serving breakfast daily from 8 AM to 11:30 AM, lunch from 1 PM to 4 PM, and dinner from 7 PM to 9 PM. With 32 rooms, including 12 suites

The pool at La Puertecita Boutique Hotel.

San Miguel's boutique hotels offer a distinctly colonial feel.

and junior suites, this is one of San Miguel's larger hotels. Rooms are furnished with either one king-sized bed or two queen-sized beds and are appointed with a rather modern Mexican décor. This hotel caters to groups such as wedding parties or business retreats. In any case, ask for special deals when making your reservation, as the hotel does offer them.

Casa Puesta del Sol (415-152-0220; www.casapuestadel sol.com) is a lush colonial B&B located on a hillside above San Miguel de Allende in a redbrick villa with vine-covered terraces that overlook the city. This space provides a magnificent view of the city and the valley beyond. Every room of this hotel has been painstakingly painted in natural colors and decorated with a wide variety of local art— including stained-glass windows and thick, colorful cotton blankets. It features four standard rooms and two suites, all decorated in an Old World Mexican style that is rich and colorful. The grounds of the hotel are beautifully landscaped with gardens, ponds, and a waterfall. Whatever they pay their gardener is probably not enough because every inch of the property seems to be manicured with great care. Guests of the hotel receive golf, swimming, tennis, and other privileges at a nearby country club. Other services include in-room salon services and tours of the city and surrounding area. Standard room rates are inexpensive to moderate while suites go for quite a bit more.

Misión de los Angeles (415-152-2099; www.hotel misiondelosangeles.com.mx) is a luxuriously appointed hotel that offers 57 rooms and suites with domed brick ceilings, and most are equipped with kitchenettes and dining rooms. They are surprisingly spacious, particularly the suites, and have balconies opening onto the pool area. The hotel architecture is distinctly colonial, with more than three hundred arches to be found throughout the property. Two stone arches tower over the hotel pool and the bar just a few feet away, where you can get a drink and relax. Adjacent to the pool is a grass area that is ideal for outdoor banquet weddings and other special occasions. The hotel is also equipped with a small gym where you can work up a sweat if you have any energy left after touring the beautiful city of San Miguel all day. The location is a little out of the way; you can take either the complimentary shuttle or a taxi into San Miguel.

Las Terrazas San Miguel (415-152-5028; www.terrazassan miguel.com) is a B&B that is actually a compound of four private casitas on a hillside overlooking San Miguel de Allende. These accommodations include a studio, a one-bedroom, and a couple of two-bedroom units—all furnished with queen-sized beds. They are decorated in a variety of styles, combining Mexican traditions with pieces from elsewhere, such as a baboon-head fountain and bamboo chairs. While this hotel doesn't have the Old World feel of some of the other B&Bs in town, the rooms are comfortably appointed and there are plenty of amenities—such as wireless high speed Internet access, cable TV, and landscaped patios. Guests are greeted with fresh flowers and a bottle of wine, as well as a gourmet breakfast each morning. Rates are set with a three-night minimum stay.

If you're looking for a room with a view, check out Casa Schuck Boutique Hotel (415-152-0657; www.casaschuck .com), a gorgeous boutique B&B located in a large 18th-century colonial villa on a hillside overlooking the city. It was restored in the 1960s by a couple of American expatriates and is now run by their granddaughter. It offers 10 spacious suites, each one uniquely decorated in styles ranging from traditional Mexican to art deco. Rooms feature private tiled bathrooms and either one king-sized or two twin-sized beds, as well as high-beamed ceilings and working fireplaces that are perfect for setting a romantic mood. Darkly colored wood and natural colors complete the effect. A full Mexican or American-style breakfast is provided. Casa Schuck also features an intimate garden swimming pool and a rooftop sundeck that provides breathtaking vistas. Located a brisk walk off the main square, this is an adults-only hotel, so leave the little ones at home if you plan on staying here. Weddings and special events can be done on the premises. Call or see their Web site for details; room rates vary significantly depending on the room.

FARTHER AFIELD

Casa de Aves (415-155-9610; www.casadeaves.com) is a retreat boutique hotel located several minutes drive outside of San Miguel. It features eight elegantly furnished private villas—each with a large bedroom, dining room, sitting area, and kitchen. These rooms are not overly decorated but are instead laid out with comfort in mind. Each of these villas is also furnished with a rooftop Jacuzzi and patio for your private enjoyment. The property is replete with amenities, and constructed in a way that makes it blend with the natural environment. Amenities include a pool with swim-up bar, a gym with yoga area, and a conference room equipped with a movie theater. There is also an on-site spa that offers facials, massages, and other services to help you unwind. Visitors can enjoy the surrounding area by taking a bird-watching hike or a ride on the mountain bikes that are provided by the hotel. For dinner, enjoy the Mexican fusion cuisine from the hotel's restaurant, open daily from 7 AM to 10 PM. No need to worry about getting into town for some sightseeing either, as the hotel offers complimentary transportation service.

Located just outside the village of Atotonílco, about 8 miles outside of San Miguel de Allende, Atotonílco el Viejo Hotel Resort & Spa (415-185-2133; www.atotonilcoelviejo .com) is one of the relatively few hotels in the area to offer resort-style lodging. This is curious, considering the nearby church for which it is named is a sanctuary and place of atonement for the poor and decrepit. The hotel itself is located in a gated compound surrounded by facilities that offer a wide variety of amenities. These include two pools (indoor and outdoor), a golf course, tennis courts, a game room, a spa, and banquet halls for special events. The on-site spa offers all kinds of services, including body exfoliation, clay wraps, and chakra therapy. The restaurant, located just off the main pool, offers indoor or outdoor service—as well as service at the palapa bar. Rooms are spacious and feature woven *bóveda* (arched) ceilings, intricately carved wooden headboards and nightstands, handmade tile floors, private balconies or terraces, and Jacuzzi bathtubs. They are furnished with one king-sized bed or two matrimonial beds.

Local Flavors

Taste of the town . . . local restaurants, bars, cafés, etc.

ON AND OFF JARDÍN ALLENDE

The busy restaurant of **Rincón de Don Tomás** (415-152-3780) is conveniently located right on Jardín Allende. The entire plaza-facing side of it is open, allowing for prime people watching while you dine. The extensive menu offers a wide range of options, the majority of which are traditional Mexican specialties; the fajitas are highly recommended. In case you're only looking for a place to relax and watch the activity of the Jardín, there is also a nice dessert and coffee menu as well as a full bar—be sure to try a fresh-squeezed margarita. The restaurant's biggest drawback, however, is that it seems to be a popular spot for smokers. Getting stuck downwind of a group puffing away is enough to make you wish you'd gone elsewhere. In any case, the food is good, the atmosphere is pleasant, the service is friendly, and the location justifies the prices—which are slightly higher than smaller nearby restaurants.

Nestled against the Parroquia, **La Capilla** (415-152-0698) offers innovative cuisine in a comfortable atmosphere. With its unbeatable view of the cathedral and mountains beyond, the rooftop terrace offers a wonderful place to dine. From red snapper in mango sauce to poblano chicken stuffed with goat cheese, most dishes are constructed around poultry and seafood and are presented in an elegant style. If you're just looking for somewhere to have a drink,

An afternoon in Jardín Allende.

there is also a piano bar here.

Café del Jardín (415-152-5006) is located on the west side of Jardín Allende. This is a great place to come and enjoy a *café con leche*. There is seating on the patio where you can sit back and plan the day's adventure. They serve all kinds of coffee and espresso drinks, along with desserts and a small selection of foods such as sandwiches, salads, and pizza. Because of its great location, it also tends to be crowded. Across the street from the Templo San Francisco, San Agustín Café (415-154-9102) is a great place to come anytime, particularly for dessert. Here, you can indulge in the Mexican tradition of *churros y chocolate*, homemade doughnuts and hot chocolate. They also serve all kinds of coffee, as well as beer, wine, and soft drinks. And, if you're in the mood for a light meal, they also have a large menu of tapas. To satisfy your sweet tooth, head to the north-east end of Jardín Allende, where **Dolphy** (415-152-2744) sells ice cream, doughnuts, coffee, and other healthy favorites. It is a great place to come on a hot afternoon.

Just 1.5 blocks east of Jardín Allende, **El Correo** (415-152-4951) specializes in a relatively small number of classic Mexican dishes. Don't expect any burritos, nachos, or chimichangas here, though—these dishes are purely old Mexico, such as *sopes* (kind of a thick tostada), moles, and enchiladas. Here, you will also find a homey ambiance. Located just 0.5 block east of Jardín Allende, it is also convenient. Reservations are accepted but not necessary.

El Pegaso Restaurant Bar (415-152-1351), located at Corregidora #6, is a casual, inviting restaurant that is a favorite among the local expatriate crowd. It is eclectically decorated with a fireplace and walls covered with work from local artists. In fact, you can buy any of it right off the wall. Breakfast is a busy time at El Pegaso, and there is good reason. They do it well, with Mexican specialties as well as dishes more standard north of the border, such as eggs Benedict, oatmeal, and lox and bagels. The lunch and dinner menu also features Mexican

dishes as well as international cuisine, with items from hamburgers to Asian specials. They also have pastrami and corned beef sandwiches as well as kung pao chicken and beef Thai salad. In addition, there is an extensive dessert menu. Drop by if you're hankering for some cheesecake, raspberry cream pie, or mile-high lemon meringue pie. For desert, head down the street to Correo #2. Here, **Dolce Capriccio** is a small Italian shop offering Italian ices, espresso drinks, and bakery treats.

West of Jardín Allende along Calle Umarán, **Pueblo Viejo** (415-152-4977; www.puebloviejo sanmiguel.com/pueblo_viejo) is a restaurant designed to offer the experience of spending a day in a 19th-century Mexican village. It is perhaps the best place in town for breakfast, with such specialties as eggs Benedict and superb blueberry pancakes—as well as dishes with a more Mexican flavor, such as *juevos rancheros* and *juevos a la Mexicana*. Upstairs, you will find La Azotea terrace bar with wonderful views of the city. Next door, you will find **Mama Mia** (415-152-2063; www.mamamia.com .mx); a popular saying among the residents of San Miguel is that you don't know this city until you've been to Mama Mia. If you're looking for a place with great atmosphere, this is a good bet, offering a wide range of menu items. From 8 AM to 1 PM, there is an inexpensive Mexican buffet breakfast as well as a nice selection of á la carte options. In the evening, the restaurant has a much more Italian flavor, with delicious specialties such as vegetarian lasagna and a variety of pastas. The restaurant has several bars that feature a variety of live music—from jazz to flamenco—and tends to attract a young crowd. And located just a few steps from Jardín Allende, it has the benefit of being convenient as well.

Casa Payo (415-152-7277), located at Zacateros #26, specializes in Argentinean-style cuisine, and that means one thing— meat. The charcoal-grilled steaks are large and tasty and there are plenty of other choices for the devoted carnivore, such as BBQ ribs and chicken. The restaurant also offers a nice wine list of national and imported flavors. Live music each night adds to the relaxed atmosphere you will find here.

If you're in the mood for some Mexican bakery treats, walk up Reloj for about a block to La Colmena Panadería (415-152-1422). Just grab a tray and load it up with whatever you want. And since Jardín Allende is just 0.5 block away, it's a perfect place to sit and enjoy your pastries.

There are many choices at the *pandelaria* (bakery).

La Finestra Caffé (415-152-5784) is located at Ancha de San Antonio #9, just a few blocks away from the Jardín. Though they do serve a light lunch, La Finestra is renowned for its interesting breakfast menu, fresh baked breads, and delicious coffee drinks. To get here, enter off the street and walk all the way through a foyer area until you get to the restaurant. The dining area is a long room that is attractively decorated, though rather narrow and slightly cramped. One side of the room is made up of leaded glass windows that overlook an attractive garden, a view that adds to the ambiance and makes this a wonderful place to start your day.

NORTH OF JARDÍN ALLENDE

North of Jardín Allende at Hidalgo #12 **Harry's New Orleans Café** (415-152-2645; www.harrysneworleanscafe.com) brings a taste of the Big Easy to old Mexico with traditional New Orleans dishes such as spicy Cajun jambalaya and seafood gumbo. The French influence doesn't stop there; the menu at Harry's is extensive, with everything from prime rib to Louisiana Rock Cornish game hen to duck. For dessert, be sure to try their chocolate truffle

Quick tip: Getting used to the food in Mexico can sometimes take a period of adjustment. A little common sense will go a long way toward making sure you don't get sick while you're enjoying yourself. You can also mitigate your chances of getting sick by eating plenty of yogurt for several weeks prior to your trip. Scientific studies have shown that the live active cultures in yogurt have properties that protect the intestinal tract from gastrointestinal infection.

cake. Needless to say, you won't find many Mexican dishes, so this is not the place for local fare. Food is served both indoors and on the patio. There is a bar that is great for hanging out with friends. Happy hour is from Monday through Friday from 5 PM to 7 PM with two-for-one martini specials all day and night on Wednesdays. Live jazz is also featured Tuesday through Thursday nights, and on Sunday evenings as well. Farther up the street is one of the more elegant Mexican restaurants in San Miguel. Unlike many restaurants in town, **Bugambilia** (415-152-

0127) offers a spacious dining area as well as an attractive patio. It has a lively, boisterous ambiance that is perfect for a night out with friends. This restaurant offers a wide-ranging menu of traditional Mexican favorites. The *chiles en nogada* (stuffed poblano chiles with walnut cream sauce) are a good bet, as is the chicken mole. And the *sopa azteca* (tortilla soup) may be the best in town. The margaritas tend to be on the strong side, and you can finish your meal by trying the homemade ice cream brought in from Dolores Hidalgo. If you plan on eating here on the weekend, it's a good idea to make reservations in advance.

If you like this . . . venture several blocks west to El Rinconcito (415-154-4809), a small family-run restaurant with an inviting atmosphere that will make you think of it as your neighborhood corner restaurant. The menu offers traditional Mexican options that are done well. Located at Refugio #7, it is a bit off the beaten path but that works to its advantage since prices here are very reasonable, and it does not have the overbearing ambiance that is synonymous with tourist traps.

Olé-Olé (415-152-0896) is a colorful restaurant tucked away several blocks north of Plaza San Francisco along Juárez. Decorated with bullfighting memorabil-ia, including several mounted bull heads, you will not mistake this place for a swanky French restaurant. The cuisine is fajitas and that's about it. Chicken, beef, shrimp, and vegetables in large portions, with a friendly staff to make sure you have a good time. Top it off with a cold beer and you have yourself a Mexican meal you won't soon forget. If the lighting is too dim in the front dining room, venture to the back of the restaurant where large skylights give the feeling of sitting in a colonial courtyard. And remember to bring cash because credit cards aren't accepted here.

Tío Lucas (415-152-1996), located at Mesones #103, is known for its live blues and jazz music that starts nightly at 9 PM. There is also live accordion music on Friday and Saturday from 3 PM to 5 PM. Though a fairly wide variety of items are on the menu, it is mainly known for its steaks, which are served in large portions. Another innovation is the house Caesar salads, which are prepared at your table in large salad bowls. It's a fun touch at first, but can take several minutes longer than the novelty lasts. This is a very good restaurant but certainly not a place to go if you are looking for an intimate evening out. The seating in the main dining room can get noisy and more than a bit cramped. Make sure you have reservations if you are planning to dine here on the weekend. The outdoor patio offers a nice alternative, with its open-air seating and over-hanging tree covered in glowing red lamps. This is a nice place to have a margarita and enjoy the music. Be warned, however, the drinks here tend to be on the strong side.

SOUTH OF JARDÍN ALLENDE

Casa del Parque (415-152-7155) is located beneath the columns of the Casa de Sierra Nevada Hotel adjacent to Parque Benito Juárez. The menu features a variety of exotic Mexican fusion specialties such as *marilú* mole and carpaccio of fresh salmon and sautéed shrimp, as well as traditional favorites such as tortilla soup and *leche quemada a la naranja* (orange-flavored burnt milk fudge). This restaurant is refined and elegant while maintaining an informal atmosphere. The patio overlooking the garden is a particularly pleasant place to enjoy lunch. There is also a bar here that is open from 1 PM to 10:30 PM. On Thursdays, it features live music from 2 PM to 4 PM and again from 8 PM to 10 PM, with Thursday night two-for-one happy hour specials running from 6 PM to 8 PM.

Three blocks west, at Jesús #23, **El Buen Café** (473-732-5807) is a wonderful little neighborhood coffee shop conveniently located near the center of town. It's mainly a breakfast restaurant, but they also do lunch as well as a variety of bakery goods. The restaurant has seating for about 40 people. Nearby, at Diez de Sollano #28, **Chimarrão** (415-154-9091) offers delicious Brazilian cuisine with an emphasis on fine meats of all sorts. You're sure to find the basics, such as beef, chicken, turkey, and pork. Additionally, you can come here to sample seasonal flavors that are not so everyday, such as lamb and rabbit. There is also a salad bar and a good wine list to complement any meal. And just around the corner at Cuadrante #5 **La Grotta** (415-152-4119) is a popular pizza restaurant that offers a couple of dining areas, including seating upstairs that has a great view of the street. That said, seating can be hard to get some nights, with the line stretching out onto the street.

At Hernández Macías #95, you will find **El Market Bistro** (415-152-3229) featuring an attractive courtyard as well as a small bar (or *Petit Bar*) with a fireplace—a nice place to have

A cobblestone street in San Miguel de Allende.

a cup of coffee during a chilly San Miguel evening. There are two menus—full and light—which offer a nice variety of options that focus on traditional French cooking, including dish-es such as chateaubriand béarnaise, tournedos montagnarde, braised sweetbreads, and salmon a la Provençale. The *Petit Bar* has a nice wine list and the courtyard offers meals with an upscale but informal feel. Live music is offered on the weekends. Next door, Romano's (415-152-7454) offers pizzas and pastas in generous portions with both indoor and outdoor dining. Pastas are made on the premises and most of the ingredients here are organ-

ic. The pizzas and bread are baked in a wood-burning oven. Being the popular place that it is, it does tend to get busy; making reservations in advance is probably a good idea. Also, remember to bring your pesos because credit cards are not accepted here.

To Do
Check out these great attractions and activities . . .

NIGHTLIFE

There are several nightlife choices west of Jardín Allende along Umarán. Among them is Bar Leonardo (415-152-2063), a small bar located in Mama Mia restaurant. It caters mainly to a young crowd, but not exclusively so. The walls are painted adobe red, with faithful recreations of famous drawings by Leonardo da Vinci. The drinks are good and strong. Try the Margarita Cadillac if you're looking for something with an extra kick. During big sporting events, crowds gather here to watch their teams play. On other nights it is flooded with young twentysome-things; don't be surprised if the girl next to you gets spontaneous and dances atop the horseshoe-shaped bar. Down the street, Berlin (415-154-9432) is a favorite among the local expatriate crowd, made up mostly of artsy Americans. It has a retractable roof and two fireplaces, so it is particularly comfortable no matter what time of the year it is. It also has a calm atmosphere and features good drinks and German food, making it a great place to start the night. Also on Umarán, Limerick Pub (415-154-8642) is a casual Irish pub with a good mix of local and international people of all ages. There are no dartboards here, but there are free pool tables. Some nights they have live music; other nights, DJs play a varied list of music. One thing that sets this

Quick tip: If you're a beer-lover looking for an interesting drink, order a *michelada.* It's a Mexican beer on ice mixed with lime juice, Clamato, and assorted peppers and spices—served in a salted glass.

San Miguel's nightlife, like everything else, is centered around Jardín Allende.

place apart from most bars in town is that they have a good selection of imported beers—Guinness on draft never tasted so amazing. Tapas y Tinis (415-154-6276) is an intimate establishment with couches and small nooks decorated with bullfighting art and old ranch implements. Overall, it has a very quiet atmosphere and is a great place to relax and have a conversation. As the name suggests, they have a menu of Spanish tapas and martinis. On Friday and Saturday nights they have live music.

A block west of Jardín Allende at Canal #16, Mechicano's (415-152-0216) is a hip club with a glitzy, modern décor. It features two bars on the main floor as well as a spectacular terrace bar upstairs. These bars offer a variety of drink specials. Occasionally, this bar stays open late on the weekend. They have live music after 8 PM or the DJ spins an assortment of dance music.

Several blocks east of Jardín Allende at San Francisco #2, Cantina la Coronela (415-154-2746) is an old-style Mexican cantina that caters to locals and travelers alike. It has a great relaxed atmosphere and traditional décor that seems right at home in this colonial city. The walls are covered with pictures of movie stars from Mexico's golden age of cinema. Nearby at Recreo #3, La Cava de la Princesa (415-152-1403) is a popular spot for the fortysomething crowd. This bar features daily live music and a small dance floor, as well as karaoke on Tuesday nights.

A block north of Jardín Allende at Mesones #97 El Caporal (415-152-5937) is a great place to come if you're looking for an authentic Mexican atmosphere. Here, live musicians play traditional ranchero songs as the crowd of locals of all ages sings along. This is a cozy, inviting place that reminds you that you're in the heart of old Mexico. For something more offbeat, head to El Ring (415-152-1998) at Hidalgo #27. This former cockfighting ring is now a large, interesting club. In addition to a large dance floor on the main level, there are also two tiers where a young, lively crowd parties late.

Guanajuato has a lively nightlife.

SHOPPING

A block off Jardín Allende along Calle Hidalgo, Exim (415-154-5282) offers a large selection of Mexican handicrafts—including candleholders, wall decorations, and furniture. The entire inventory here is handmade of ceramic, glass, and other materials. A bit farther down the street, Bacara (415-152-0062) sells high-quality leather goods—including bags, boots, belts, and jackets. Most of their stock comes from the nearby city of León; they also have a selection of watches. Just a block over at Reloj #12, in a building adorned with sculpted gargoyles, Productos Herco (415-152-1434) has a range of items to help you redecorate and remodel your bathroom and kitchen. This includes iron door knockers, pewter bowls, cast brass washbasins, and plenty of *talavera* trays and plates. They also have a selection of wood and wrought-iron furniture.

West of Jardín Allende at Canal #21, Cerroblanco (415-154-4888) offers an array of fine silver and gold jewelry. Many pieces are embossed with precious and semiprecious stones. It is run by third generation jewelry designers who design all of their own pieces. The work has been sold at Nordstom and Saks Fifth Avenue stores. A block away at Umarán #17, Lagundi (415-152-7395) has a selection of art books and English-language magazines.

Another place to find some reading is south of Jardín Allende at Sollano #30. Here, El Colibrí (415-152-0751) offers a selection of

There's plenty of shopping to do in San Miguel.

Did you know?

Talavera is a colorful form of earthenware that was brought to Mexico by Spanish guild artisans during the 16th century. These Spanish artisans blended their techniques with those of Mexico's indigenous populations, who already had long traditions of firing earthenware that went back centuries. Ceramics covered with intricate blue-and-white designs are emblematic of the older Spanish tradition. Mexican indigenous artisans later added multi-colored floral, celestial, and other motifs. Unfortunately, *talavera* is notorious for being made with glazes with high lead content. Therefore, if you plan to use your *talavera* for anything besides decorative purposes, you should buy it from the more reputable artisans who guarantee that their work meets U.S. standards.

English-language paperbacks and magazines. Nearby Camila (415-152-2697) specializes in etched glass flatware as well as tablecloths, linens, and an assortment of other decorative household accessories. Sollano 16 (415-154-8872; www.sollano16.com) is located in a beautiful colonial building with a large courtyard. They sell a variety of luxury goods including textiles, furniture, jewelry, and other accessories. They have a variety of antiques as well. Much of their inventory is imported from Europe, South America, and other exotic locations.

Talavera comes in many forms.

Also south of Jardín Allende at Jesús #11, you will find Libros el Tecolote (415-152-7395), a small boutique bookstore with a nice selection of English-language books, including guide-books, books on the arts and architecture, and children's books. At Recreo #36, Galería Mariposa (415-152-4488) sells

Traditional Mexican dancer dolls made from corn husks.

traditional Mexican folk art from around the country. Among the items you will find here are Oaxacan *alebríjes,* carved animal figurines that are sometimes monstrous and always intricately painted with minute dot patterns. This shop also has a small number of works by local painters. Caracol Collection (415-152-1617) is located at Cuadrante #30. This shop features a collection of fine and applied arts by Mexican artists and artisans from around the country, and includes clothing and furniture. The collection exhibits many different traditions, with pieces made of materials such as paper, silver, wood, and clay. At Hernández Macías #110, Zócalo Mexican Folk Art (415-152-0663; www.zocalotx.com) sells a wide variety of Mexican folk art from around the country. This includes highly traditional items such as *talavera*, clay Katrina (female skeleton) Day of the Dead figurines, and Oaxacan *alebríjes.* You will also find more hard-to-find items here as well, such as carved masks and engraved glassware.

There are plenty of interesting finds for anyone who wants to explore a little farther off the beaten path. Several blocks north of Jardín Allende, along Calzada de la Aurora, you will find many fine shops. Among them, Surfaces (415-152-2068; www.ceramicaantique

Alebrijes are traditional Oaxacan wood carvings.

.com) is a tile shop that manufactures and sells a wide variety of high-quality handcrafted Mexican tiles. They have styles that include Mexican, Moroccan, and Italian, and have an interactive design display as well as a large tile gallery. They do custom orders and have a knowledgeable staff on hand for consultations. Down the street, **Buenas Noches** (415-154-9624) is an interesting bath shop owned and run by a couple of American expatriates. It stocks a range of imported and Mexican bath and bedroom furnishings, including Egyptian bedsheets and comforters; large, soft bath towels; and scented soaps and candles. Another fine shop along Calzada de la Aurora is **Finca Home** (415-154-8323; www.rachelhorn.com). This shop stocks hand-finished wrought-iron and wood furniture such as armoires, chests, and end tables. They also offer imported leather furniture, a selection of wrought-iron and copper light fixtures and lighting accessories, and imported fabrics. **Casa de las Artesenias de Michoacán** (415-155-9211) is run by a nonprofit organization associated with the Mexican state of Michoacán. They specialize in selling folk art from that state, including ceramics, wood carvings, copper goods, and furniture.

A local artisan crafting his wares. Maria Miller Kisska

At Ignacio Cruces #4, San Miguel Designs (415-150-0058; www .sanmigueldesigns.com) sells clothing with prints that are steeped in Mexican culture. This includes items such as kimonos and shower curtains adorned with the image of the Virgin of Guadalupe, shirts and aprons peppered with Day of the Dead skeletons, and other such items. If you are looking for interesting jewelry creations, check out Kelli Brown Jewelry (415-154-7069; www.kellibrownjewelry.com). Raised in Austin, Texas, the daughter of a noted architectural designer and an art dealer, Kelli Brown grew up with a passion for design and beauty. Today, she creates bold jewelry in gold and silver with precious and semiprecious stones. The result is an Old World feel of booty from a pirate's chest. The shop is located in a hacienda that is more than three hundred years old. Call for an appointment and Kelli will even arrange for you to be picked up from your hotel. More quality jewelry creations can be found high above Jardín Allende at Tanque #14. Here you will find Piedras (415-154-9193; www.piedras sanmiguel.com), a jewelry store run by an American expatriate and a San Miguel native. It features jewelry made of beautiful semiprecious stones such as freshwater pearls, Mexican fire opal, and jade—as well as less traditional materials, such as petrified wood. They use these materials to make earrings and bracelets—and thick, draping necklaces with a distinctive Mexican feel.

ARCHITECTURAL HERITAGE

During the three centuries of Spanish rule, San Miguel de Allende was basically constructed from the ground up following the path of Spanish architecture. Beginning with Gothic—then moving on to Renaissance, followed by baroque, and finally

Quick tip: Contrary to what you were taught in high school Spanish, if you want to know how much something costs, try not to say *"¿Cuanto cuesta?"* This is a dead giveaway that you're a gringo, meaning that you've probably just added a few pesos to the price of the item. Instead say *"¿A cuanto?"* This phrase just might pass you off as a *chilango* (Mexico City resident), making the vendor think that you are wise to inflated prices.

ending with neoclassical—the architecture of this region can be traced back to the preferences of Spanish architects. However, structures also display distinct local variations, such as the signature pastel-colored stucco of Guanajuato and the pale pink stone of San Miguel's churches, which infuse the predominantly Spanish architecture with a markedly regional flair.

During the colonial period, San Miguel was home to one of the most prosperous populations in all of New Spain. Furthermore, when the region's silver-mining resources were first discovered in 1558, and the settlement that sprung up around these mines immediately began to flourish, it was during the period of transition between Renaissance and baroque architecture. The Spanish had tapped what turned out to be one of the world's most productive silver veins, and it filled silver barons' pockets. This surge of wealth set off a boom in construction that provided both Guanajuato and San Miguel with the graceful mansions and arresting churches and plazas that continue to provide visitors and residents alike with enchanting public spaces.

The Renaissance was truly a period of rebirth of ancient cultural, artistic, and architectural ideals, as it drew from the Roman and Greek traditions. In Mexico, this movement generally manifested

The Parroquia de San Miguel is one of Mexico's most unique churches.

itself in the form of plateresque. *Plata* being the Spanish word for silver, this branch of the Renaissance style earned its name because it was particularly ornamental and thought to resemble decorative silverwork. Plateresque is predominantly known for the sculpted stone of its façades and doorways, which are still considered important elements of architecture in San Miguel de Allende.

In the early 17th century, the baroque architectural style began to become fashionable in San Miguel. Where the Renaissance style emphasized the balance of classic shapes like circles, squares, and triangles, the baroque style integrated elements like curves, contrasts of light and shadow, color, and elaborate decoration for a more dramatic impact. This movement also incorporated other artistic elements such as ornate and massive altarpieces. Churrigueresque, a specific form of the baroque, peaked in Mexico between 1730 and 1780. Constructions from this period boast amazingly elaborate decoration. You can see quintessential examples of this in the façades of the Templo San Francisco and La Campañia de Jesús in Guanajuato.

In the 18th century, the neoclassical period brought another change of tastes with a return to the simplicity, harmony, and sobriety of the early Greek and Roman civilizations. Guanajuato's best example of this would probably be the plain blocklike structure of the Alhóndiga de Granaditas. It was also during this time that Zeferino Gutiérrez gave San Miguel's Parroquia its Gothic façade, which has come to symbolize the city itself.

San Miguel de Allende has an old-world feel.

West of the Parroquia, you will find Museo Histórico de San Miguel de Allende (415-152-2499) in a two-story colonial house that was once owned by the city's prominent de Allende and Unzaga families. This museum is dedicated to Don Ignacio Allende, who fought and died for Mexican independence, and the man for whom the city is partially named. It features a historic collection of weapons, documents, and other objects either belonging to the leader or pertaining to the Mexican War for Independence. It also has a few pieces of contemporary art. In one corner of the museum you will find a sculpture of Allende. A plaque in the façade says *AQUI NACIO EL CONOCIDA EN TODAS PARTES* (roughly translated as "Born here, known everywhere").

In 1873, construction was completed on Teatro Ángela Peralta (415-152-7599), a neoclassical theater that was meant to be a modest concert hall for the residents of San Miguel. Coincidentally, the famous soprano singer Ángela Peralta happened to be traveling through Guanajuato at the time. She accepted an invitation to come to San Miguel and was received with a grand procession. She gave several performances in the theater, and in 1881 she returned to have the theater reinaugurated in her name. The theater continues to be a center for art and performances. Today, the theater hosts a variety of plays, ballet, and lectures, among other cultural activities.

A statue of Don Ignacio Allende outside of Museo Histórico de San Miguel de Allende.

Galleries

San Miguel de Allende is without a doubt one of North America's most significant artist colonies. For almost a century it has been a place where artists come to dedicate themselves to their art. Its rich colonial

There are many galleries to choose from in San Miguel de Allende.

atmosphere has inspired these artists to go beyond themselves to create works they didn't know they were capable of. Consequently, the town is replete with galleries selling original works of art by local artists. These galleries range from the modest to the luxurious, and prices range just as much. You will find art here by both unknown local indigenous artists and established painters with works in galleries worldwide. Works run the gamut from watercolors to hand-pounded copper pieces. What is wonderful is that you are free to evaluate and enjoy the work as you wish. Furthermore, more often than not, you will have the opportunity to interact with these amazing individuals that have put so much of themselves into their work. What follows is only a small sampling of what you will find here.

The William Martin Gallery (415-152-5282; www.williammartin gallery.com) is located in an old colonial home in the heart of San Miguel. It features the work of a small number of artists. Their work runs from portraits and landscapes to abstract works. Private and semi-private art classes with William Martin may also be arranged by contacting the gallery or by going to their Web site. Nearby, Galería Arte Sacro (415-152-3292; www.galeriasartesacro.com.mx) specializes in portraits of Catholic saints. The portraits are painted in a style of painting that was popular in the colonial period and became widespread among native artists in Peru in the 17th century. The subjects are painted in the foreground, often wearing highly stylized costumes, and usually with a scenic view of a landscape or a town in the background.

Galería Pérgola (415-154-5595; www.galeriapergola.com) offers a large collection of works of various artists from throughout Mexico. A large variety of styles and mediums are available. It is located in a complex of the landmark school Instituto Allende, the summer home of the prominent 17th century Canal family, the patron family of San Miguel. This gallery opened here in 1951 as an exhibit space for Instituto Allende. The building has gone through renovation and now features vaulted ceilings and light-filled spaces that mix with colonial

The religious art of Galería Arte Sacro.

architecture. The work here is of high quality and eclectic, and easily interesting enough to warrant a look even if you're not in the market for fine art. **Juan Ezcurdia Gallery** (415-152-6539; www.ezcurdia .com) features the work of highly acclaimed Mexican artist Juan Ezcurdia. He is a self-taught painter who paints colorful works with a fanciful flair. He won the National Illustration Prize in 1997 and now has works in private collections all over the world.

Sacred Sites

The **Parroquia de San Miguel** (The Parish of St. Michael the Archangel) towers over Jardín Allende. With its jutting vertical lines and intricately carved spires, it is one of the most distinctive churches in Mexico—and that is saying something. It has come to be the symbol of San Miguel and is dedicated to Friar Juan de San Miguel, the founder of the city. However, this distinctive work of architecture is not a cathedral, but rather a parish church. It was originally built in the 17th century with a baroque façade and three high towers. In the late 19th century, the indigenous Mexican architect Zeferino Gutiérrez radically changed the façade to the Gothic structure that you see today. During special occasions, the church is lit up at night with colorful spotlights, giving it even more of an illusory appearance. A

The Parroquia de San Miguel can be seen from all over San Miguel.

plaque in the entrance of the parish proclaims the attendance of a few former priests—LOS CURAS MIGUEL AND JOSÉ JOAQUIN HIDALGO OFRECIERON MISA EN ESTE TEMPLO, 1748 (The priests Miguel and José Joaquin Hidalgo offered mass in this church, 1748). The church also produces the loudest regular sound in the city, with church bells that are nearly 6 feet high and 8.5 inches thick.

The church's interior has been remodeled on more than one occasion over the years and presents a diverse range of objects and decorations from a variety of periods and styles. The neoclassical altars blend with murals by Federico Cantú that depict not only religious topics but make social commentary as well. These murals were considered so radical when they were completed that a parish priest tried to have them destroyed. To the left, you will find the chapel of the Señor de la Conquista with the figure of the Cristo de la Conquista. This highly revered 16th-century statue was sculpted by Indians in the city of Pátzcuaro, Michoacán, and is constructed of a paste of maize stalks stuck together with a gum made from orchid tubers and coated with chalk. Other religious artwork within the parish includes the image of Saint Michael the Archangel on one of the altarpieces, as well as a statue of Christ in the vestry that was designed by the religious sculptor Fidias Elizondo. Former president Anastasio Bustamante is buried in the basement (though his heart is in Mexico City) in a crypt that is open to the public during Day of the Dead. On Sunday, masses are held on the hour from 6 AM to 1 PM and again at 6 PM and 8:15 PM.

Just northeast of Jardín Allende, at the corner of Juárez and San Francisco, you will find Templo San Francisco, a church that appears to be much more dated than the Parroquia. In fact it is, with a connected chapel (known as the Chapel of the Third Order) dating all the way back to 1713. The main building is the convent church of San Francisco, which was constructed with donations from wealthy families and funds from bullfights. Construction began in 1779, and it was finished 20 years later by the architect Francisco Eduardo

Tresguerras. It has an intricate churrigueresque façade with a lofty neoclassical tower. In front of the church is a small courtyard containing a monument to Christopher Columbus. Inside are nine altars and a neoclassical interior with paintings depicting the death of St. Francis. On Sunday, masses are held at 7:15 AM, 10:30 AM, noon, 6 PM, and 7:15 PM.

A few blocks north you will find the **Templo de Nuestra Señora de la Salud** (Church of Our Lady of Health), which faces Plaza Civica. It dates back to the 18th century and was commissioned by Father Luis Felipe Neri de Alfaro to be used as the chapel of the prestigious School of San Francisco de Sales. The interior is a Latin cross layout decorated with sev-

The concave abocinada entrance of the Templo de Nuestra Señora de la Salud.

eral oil paintings from prominent 18th-century artists, including several by Agapito Ping. This church features a dome covered with bright yellow and blue tile and an unfinished tower that houses the oldest bell in the city. It is also one of only six churches in Mexico with a concave *abocinada* entrance, which is in the shape of a carved conch shell with a single eye inside a triangle. This symbolizes the omnipresence of God; however, there is also a local belief that this is actually because the church has the power to cure eye ailments.

At Insurgentes #12, you will find the **Oratorio de San Felipe Neri**. This chapel was built by the local indigenous population in the early 18th century and, physically speaking, it is best known for its many domes of different shapes and sizes. It was commissioned by the priest Juan Antonio Pérez de Espinoza from Pátzcuaro, Michoacán, who came to San Miguel for a short visit in 1712—and ended up staying. This is the most indigenous-influenced church in San Miguel de Allende. Although it has gone through several restorations, the original façade of pink stone is still present on the eastern side of the church, along with a small statue of *Nuestra Señora de Soledad* (Our Lady of Solitude). The southern exterior exhibits a much newer baroque façade. In the interior of the church are more than 30 oil paintings attributed to Miguel Cabrera that depict the life of San Felipe Neri, the Italian saint who founded the congregation of the Oratorio. There is an adjoining chapel to the Oratorio de San Felipe Neri called Santa Casa de Loreto. This chapel was commissioned by the Canal family in 1736 and is a reproduction of the Santa Casa de Loreto in Loreto, Italy. To enter this chapel, go up the left aisle of the Oratorio to the front of the church and turn left. It has a small baroque nave covered with gold leaf and an altar dominated by a painting of the Virgen de Loreto.

Directly west of Jardín Allende, the Templo de la Concepcion (Church of the Immaculate Conception) is best known as "Templo de Las Monjas" (Church of the Nuns) because it originally belonged to the Order of the Immaculate Conception. Its size was considered excessive for the number of nuns that occupied it in the second half of the 18th century, which some historians have put at around eight. The funds for this church were put up by Josefa de la Canal, daughter of Don Manuel Tomás de la Canal, one of the city's great benefactors. Construction on this church was begun in 1755 by the architect Francisco Martinez Gudiño and, like the Parroquia, it was completed by Zeferino Gutiérrez in the 19th century. In 1891, Gutiérrez added a dome that was inspired by the Church of Saint-Louis des Invalides in Paris. This building also briefly housed an art school in the 1960s. The

Did you know?

Legend has it that in 1910, when the Mexican Revolution was in full swing, many churches in the region were under constant threat by looters intent on stealing gold objects and other valuables. In order to hide their gold and religious artifacts, the priests bought a young bull from a local farmer. They slaughtered this bull and removed its organs, replacing them with their treasure. They then buried the bull underneath the altar of the Oratorio de San Felipe Neri. It is said that this bull is still buried there today, although there is no discernible evidence of this.

The interior of the Templo de la Concepcion.

church's spacious atrium allows you to admire its enormous neoclassical interior, which is decorated with baroque sculptures that frame the doors, and a collection of paintings by famous artists such as Miguel Cabrera and Juan Rodriguez Juárez. Sunday masses are offered in English at 10 AM.

Language Schools

Academia Hispano Americana (415-152-0349; www.ahaspeakspanish .com) has been operating in San Miguel since 1959. They offer a comprehensive Spanish immersion program, as well as a semi-intensive program and one-on-one courses. The school's courses are divided into 12 four-week sessions that roughly correspond with the months of the year. There are no classes in late December or early January, or in late March or early April. This school prefers that you stay with a local family during your stay. They will arrange this when you enroll. However, if you choose to stay elsewhere, you must make your own arrangements. Check their Web site for specific dates. Open Monday through Friday from 8 AM to 7 PM.

Centro Bilingue (415-152-5400; www.centrobilingue.com) offers intensive or conversation-level Spanish courses for business professionals or just those who would like to learn another language. The faculty of the school will evaluate you upon arrival to determine your level of proficiency and course needs. They will also help to arrange for you to stay with local families during your stay in San Miguel. There are special seasonal courses for children during the winter, spring break, and summer seasons. Private lessons can also be arranged.

Centro Mexicano de Lengua y Cultura de San Miguel (415-152-0763; www

Quick tip: If you are traveling to Guanajuato or San Miguel to study Spanish, be sure to investigate several schools to find out what they can offer in terms of accommodations as well as their curriculum. The majority of these schools prefer their students take lodging with local families in order to facilitate Spanish immersion. Rates for these types of accommodations usually cover several home-cooked meals with your host family every day. This can save you money and will certainly give you plenty of exposure to everyday Mexican culture.

.josefinaschool.com) offers Spanish classes at varying levels of proficiency, from the very basic to the very advanced. As part of their curriculum, they go out into the community to introduce their students to different aspects of San Miguel that ordinary tourists usually don't see, such as hospitals, churches, and factories. They will help you make arrangements for accommodations, though they recommend that you stay with a local family. They also offer private sessions, as well as a special program for children. This program is geared toward children between the ages of 3 and 12, and involves weekday classes of four-hour sessions.

Instituto de Habal Hispana (415-152-0713; www.mexicospanish .com) focuses on intensive immersion Spanish classes for adult learn-

The craftsmen that built San Miguel built it to last centuries.

Creativity is everywhere in San Miguel.

ers. These classes include learning songs, taking walks through San Miguel, and even Mexican cooking lessons. They take students with beginner through advanced Spanish skills, with courses that run up to four weeks. See their Web site for specific dates. They will help you make arrangements for staying with a local family or at a hotel, and they can also help you with renting an apartment.

Warren Hardy Spanish School (415-154-4017; www .warrenhardy.com) specializes in teaching adult language learners with beginning to proficient level Spanish needs. They also offer a complete series of books and CDs for their learn-at-home program. The on-site courses in San Miguel are two and a half weeks long, with classes meeting for three hours per day, three days per week. These courses are designed to teach you to speak Spanish in the Mexican dialect, with an emphasis on Mexican culture. Classes rotate throughout the year, with many focusing on different aspects of Spanish conjugation and tenses. See their Web site for the schedule of classes.

Art Classes

For nearly a century now, art has been the cultural element that has made San Miguel de Allende thrive. Before it was known as an enclave for expatriates or restaurateurs, it was a burgeoning artists' colony. In fact it was the opportunity this town presented, of learning from its artists, which resulted in such an international community. These opportunities still exist today in San Miguel de Allende. Of course, the two main schools of Bellas Arts and Instituto Allende are still in operation, offering classes on such diverse subjects as photography, ceramics, and dance. But there are also plenty of other outlets offering classes that are perhaps more personalized and less

It is not hard to see why San Miguel has inspired many artists.

structured. Many of the graduates of San Miguel's great art schools have stayed in the city and set up schools of their own. If you plan on staying in town for an extended period, there is a wide range of options for whatever medium you are interested in. If you plan to be here for just a day, or even a few hours, there are certainly schools here to accommodate you.

Bellas Artes (415-152-0289), also known as El Nigromante, has a storied history. It has its roots in the first school established by Felipe Cossío del Pomar in 1937. It is located one block off Jardín Allende. It offers monthly classes on a wide variety of artistic mediums, including drawing, painting, sculpture, photography, and ceramics— as well as music, ballet, and dance. Classes begin on the first of the month and children are admitted at half price. Another one of San Miguel's historic art schools is Instituto Allende (415-152-0190; www .instituto-allende.edu.mx). This institution began offering classes in

1951. It is located in a large colonial building and offers courses in such subjects as painting, drawing, sculpture, ceramics, and art history; it also offers a Spanish program. This is an accredited institution offering academic credits and even MFA degrees. Many of its students have gone on to set up art studios here in San Miguel de Allende. Classes run year-round.

If you're looking for a more personal experience, consider Classes Unlimited (415-154-5366; www.classesunlimited.com). Despite its name, instructors keep class size limited, offering personalized instruction in a variety of subjects, including photography, writing, and fine arts; drawing and painting classes are available for children age six and older. At Edina Sagert Studio (415-120-8088; www.edina sagert.com), year-round but intermittent watercolor classes are intensive but are appropriate for both beginners and advanced students. Edina Sagert is a German-born artist who has lived and traveled all over the world, including India, Southeast Asia, and the United States. Keith Keller's La Escuela (415-152-0637; www.casadesuenos mexico.com) offers classes in drawing and painting. He provides students with personal instruction and unlimited access to two studios that open onto a garden courtyard. Beginners generally start by learning to draw simple forms and then move on to figurative drawing. More experienced artists generally paint as they wish and receive critique, or learn techniques such as glazing. Registration is not required and materials can be purchased in Mexico.

Cooking Classes

Over the last 30 years, San Miguel de Allende's reputation as an international center of culture has grown to include the culinary arts. As local cooks have found a market in cooking classes and as international restaurateurs have settled here, cooking vacations have become a cottage industry. These knowledgeable chefs teach their students the time-honored techniques of classical Mexican cuisine. And best of all, when the class is over, you get to eat the results. These cooking classes are usually combined with cultural excursions in which you learn about the city and the surrounding environs. Often, this will include jaunts to Guanajuato to take a look at the town's highlights. Moreover, these cooking vacations result in an experience that you can share with friends and family in a way that they will thank you for. What follows is just a few of the opportunities you will find in San Miguel de Allende.

Hugh Carpenter is the author of 16 cookbooks and has been teaching cooking for more than 30 years. While he is based in California, he offers weeklong cooking courses in San Miguel de Allende from January through March at **Hugh Carpenter Cooking School** (707-252-9773; www.hughcarpenter .com). Carpenter is well known for his laid-back and amiable personality, and in his courses students learn the art of Mexican cuisine in a variety of venues and meet several of the local artists living in San Miguel. Activities include wine tasting, hands-on cooking, and cultural events.

San Miguel has narrow sidewalks where it has any at all.

Culinary Adventures of Mexico (415-154-4825; www .mexicocooks.com) is run by Kris Rudolph, also the owner of El Buen Café. Rudolf is the author of three cookbooks and has been teaching cooking in San Miguel de Allende since 1996. She offers a variety of classes including Naturally Healthy Mexican Cuisine, Modern Mexican Fusion, Market Tour, and Salsa Cooking.

The Arcos del Atascadero B&B offers weeklong courses at **Mexican Cooking Vacation** (415-152-5299; www.mexicancookingvacation .com). Students are taught a variety of classic Mexican dishes as well as cake decorating, and receive guided tours of sites such as the people's market, Guanajuato, and Dolores Hidalgo. Classes are taught by María Marquez, who has taught such celebrity chefs as Rick Bayless.

Nancy Zaslavsky is the author of two cookbooks and has been traveling throughout Mexico and exploring its cuisine since 1970. At **A Cook's Tour of San Miguel de Allende** (310-440-8877; www .nancyzaslavsky.com), she offers a weeklong tour of San Miguel de Allende in February, in which she guides foodies through the culinary highlights of San Miguel de Allende and Guanajuato. Tour members stay at a restored colonial B&B in the heart of downtown San Miguel, and will take tours on such things as cheese and tequila making as well as several cooking classes.

Traditional Mexican Cooking School (415-152-4376; www.tradi tionalmexicancooking.com.mx) is run by Marilau Ricaud, who belongs to a family that boasts several generations of Mexican cooks. She teaches students how to make traditional dishes from all over Mexico, including mole poblano, tamales, and pazole. Classes are Monday through Friday beginning at 10 am, and run approximately three hours.

Tours

Polanco Tours (415-152-4193; www.internetsanmiguel.com/polanco/ polanco.htm) offers transportation to and from the León airport. They also offer art tours by appointment that cover scenic and his- toric sights in San Miguel, Atotonílco, Dolores Hidalgo, the ghost mining town of Pozos, and Guanajuato. You can also schedule cook- ing classes with this company to learn about the fine art of authentic Mexican cooking. Gonzalez Tours and Transportation (415-152- 5552; http://transportesgonzalez.tripod.com) offers private transporta- tion to the León airport for up to eight people. You can also arrange for transport to and from locations such as Querétaro, Guadalajara, and Mexico City. They even offer chauffeur service to the United States. They also offer a variety of historic tours in San Miguel and the surrounding cities.

If it's an adventure that you're looking for, check out Coyote Canyon Adventures (415-154-4193; www.coyotecanyonadventures .com). This tour group is located on a ranch about 10 miles outside of San Miguel de Allende. They offer several kinds of tours and excur- sions, including horseback riding, hiking, mountain biking, ATV adventures, and even hot air balloon rides. Another unique tour group is LifePath Spa Retreats (415-154-8465; www.lifepathretreats .com), a center for personal growth and healing. This organization offers lectures, classes, workshops, and retreats devoted to wellness of the body, mind, and spirit. They offer a quiet atmosphere of deep reflection where professionals offer psychological and spiritual guid- ance. It is staffed with trained individuals with years of experience specializing in psychology, Oriental medicine, counseling, and mas- sage therapy. They also feature visiting practitioners and personal growth special events.

2

Guanajuato

GUANAJUATO IS FIRST and foremost thought of as a historic colonial city. However, the city has a lively energy that comes from its university. It was the university that took over the Teatro Principal after years of neglect—and the university students who sowed the seeds that would eventually grow into the Cerventino Festival. And it has been the presence of this young crowd that has made the city a popular weekend destination, despite the fact that there isn't a beach within miles. Young people are a constant feature here and they give the place a spirited atmosphere that is creative and intellectual, offering visitors an enlightened experience against the backdrop of old Mexico.

Pick Your Spot

Best places to stay in Guanajuato, and what you'll find nearby . . .

COLONIAL CENTER

Without a doubt one Guanajuato's most charming features—as well as a big reason why it was designated a UNESCO world heritage site in 1988 (and the entire town as a national monument in 1926)—is the fact that the colonial center is dominated by a series of charming plazas, each with its own look and feel. Chief among these plazas is the triangular Jardín de la Unión, which is truly

LEFT: El Pípila viewed from Jardín de la Unión.

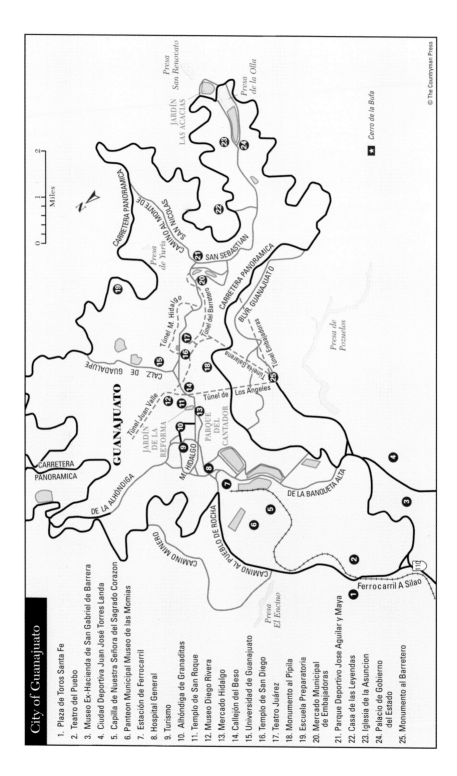

City of Guanajuato

1. Plaza de Toros Santa Fe
2. Teatro del Puebo
3. Museo Ex-Hacienda de San Gabriel de Barrera
4. Ciudad Deportiva Juan José Torres Landa
5. Capilla de Nuestra Señora del Sagrado Corazon
6. Panteon Municipal Museo de las Momias
7. Estación de Ferrocarril
8. Hospital General
9. Turismo
10. Alhóndiga de Granaditas
11. Templo de San Roque
12. Museo Diego Rivera
13. Callejón del Beso
14. Teatro Juárez
15. Universidad de Guanajuato
16. Templo de San Diego
17. Teatro Juárez
18. Monumento al Pipila
19. Escuela Preparatoria
20. Mercado Municipal de Embajadoras
21. Parque Deportivo Jose Aguilar y Maya
22. Casa de las Leyendas
23. Iglesia de la Asuncion
24. Palacio de Gobierno del Estado
25. Monumento al Barretero

© The Countryman Press

the heart of the city. In colonial times (before there was a Mexican union), this plaza was called the Plaza San Diego, because it served mainly as the front courtyard of the Templo San Diego. At that time it was bare of trees and it doubled as an outdoor market and, at times, even a bullfighting ring. In 1836 a row of trees was planted, but the plaza as it is today did not start to take shape until the 1860s—when the main gardens were planted, benches were installed, and cobblestone walkways were laid around the perimeter. At this time it was rechristened Jardín de la Unión. Today, locals and visitors alike gather here to enjoy the shade of its manicured Indian laurel trees and listen to the music of the mariachis or the *estudiantina* minstrels. On Thursdays and Sundays at around 7 PM the plaza's central bandstand comes alive with the music of the state band.

While the east side is lined with a variety of shops, the south end of the plaza is where you will find the Templo San Diego and the famed Teatro Juárez. These are popular staging grounds for street theater and display areas for local artists. To the west of the Templo San Diego, you will find the Hotel San Diego (473-732-1300; www.hotelsandiegogto.com.mx). This is an old and historic hotel, as can be seen in the murals right off the lobby, which depict the building during its colonial days. This hotel features 43 comfortably appointed suites—though there is nothing particularly special about the décor of the rooms. They range from singles to quadruples to junior suites. However, before you get excited about the prospects of its convenient location, it's important to remember that Guanajuato is a college town that loves to stay up late.

The Hotel San Diego.

Quick tip: If you're staying in the Hotel San Diego during a weekend or festival, forget the view and request a room in the hotel's interior. The rooms along the exterior can be extremely loud *all night*. This is particularly true if you're unfortunate enough to get stuck with a room facing Alonso, the street that runs along the back of the hotel.

Along the west side of Jardín de la Unión, you will find a row of hotels with restaurants that feature patio seating that opens onto the plaza. Among these is the Hotel Luna (473-732-9725; www.hotelluna.com.mx). This hotel is located in a 19th-century building and has been operating for more than one hundred years. In fact, it provided accommodations for Porfirio Díaz, the Mexican president, when he came to Guanajuato in 1903 to inaugurate Teatro Juárez. It offers 19 rooms and 2 suites; they are comfortable and elegant, even if they are somewhat small. Some rooms have a balcony with views of the Jardín de la Unión, but you might want to resist the urge to take one of these rooms if you are in town during a busy weekend; instead,

request a room away from the square to avoid the noise. With each night's stay breakfast is included at the Restaurante Conde Rul, which is located on the hotel's ground floor facing the Jardín. The hotel also offers complimentary service to and from the León airport. Not having to worry about arranging an early morning taxi will put your mind at ease and allow you to enjoy the beautiful surroundings.

Next door, you will find the Posada Santa Fe (473-732-0084; www.posada-santafe.com). This hotel has been around since the 1860s and is probably the oldest hotel in Guanajuato. Having survived all that history, it is also one of the most attractive hotels in the city. It has on display an admirable collection of works from the local artist and historian Manuel Leal. The lobby is impressive, with chandeliers hanging from a high beamed ceiling, and antique chairs below giant paintings. Off the lobby is the hotel restaurant and lounge—a great place to have a drink and take in the atmosphere. The hotel's 40 rooms and 9 suites are located up a winding staircase. Standard rooms tend to be small but they are well maintained and comfortable. The suites have fancier furniture and exterior views of the Jardín. Breakfast is included in the room rate for each night's stay.

Walk out the north end of Jardín de la Unión and veer to the left and you will come upon a small square called Plazuela Baratillo. It is surrounded by colorful colonial buildings; in the center of the plaza is a beautiful Florentine fountain adorned with sculpted fish at the base. This fountain was a royal gift from a French princess—at one time it sat in the Plaza de la Paz, but was transferred here in 1893 to make room for the Monumento a la Paz. However, this plaza does not take its name from anything so regal as the fountain. In the 19th century there was a market here where vendors would yell *"barato!"*—assuring prospective customers that their wares were cheap. Hence, residents took to calling it *baratillo* and the name stuck. Just north of this plaza, you will find La Casa Azul (473-731-2288; www.lacasaazul.com.mx). This attractive boutique hotel is located in a quiet neighborhood just a few blocks north of the town center. It features three large rooms with sitting areas. They are decorated in a sparse Mexican hacienda style that is both warm and inviting. The rest of the hotel is as simple and lovely as the rooms and has an atmosphere that takes you back to Guanajuato's colonial days. There is a small garden area with a stone fountain just in front of a small chapel. There is also a cantina with bare brick

Plazuela Baratillo.

Quick tip: Be sure to pack some comfortable walking shoes and be prepared to walk up a lot of stairs during your stay (and this is not just limited to your hotel). Most of the more interesting hotels are located in buildings that are at least a century old and do not have elevators (though larger hotels away from the city center do have elevators). Furthermore, the city is located on the side of a mountain and several of the hotels are actually built into the side of it. Though you'll undoubtedly see local women wearing them, this is not a town that has been constructed with high heels in mind.

walls, dim lighting, and rustic wooden furniture. Sitting here, you almost get the feeling that you should've brought your six-shooter. However, you may find yourself spending the most time on the hotel's rooftop terrace, which has plenty of shade and a beautiful panoramic view of the city.

To the west, along Calle Positos, you will find several other hotels that are far enough away from the crowd noise to offer a cozy retreat while at the same time providing a convenient home base near the city center. The best of these is the **Mesón de los Poetas** (473-732-6657; www.mesondelospoetas .com). This charming hotel is one of the best-known hotels in Guanajuato. Located in a cavernous house built into a hill-side just down the street from the Diego Rivera Museum, it

offers 30 rooms that are uniquely decorated—each dedicated to poets from Walt Whitman to Pablo Neruda. They all feature original paintings and Mexican décor. Rooms are furnished with two double beds or a double and a twin, and suites have king-sized beds. They are also equipped with a kitchenette and a sitting area. The hotel's position against a hillside keeps the rooms quiet unless there is an antsy woman in high heels situated in the room above you (as happened to me one morning). Be prepared to walk a lot of stairs if you stay here because there are plenty of them. A continental breakfast is provided with each night's stay.

A long block south, along Avenida Juárez, you will find the **Mesón del Rosario** (473-732-0666) a good option for the budget traveler who is seeking a

Inside the Mesón del los Poetas hotel in Guanajuato.

no-frills hotel that is also close to the center of the action. Just a standard room with a TV on the wall that gets a few Spanish-language channels, but you can spend a lot more and do much worse (and I have). Originally built to house miners, there is something cavernous about this hotel. Entering it, you are greeted by an old suit of armor that stands guard over a small sitting area—but what is most striking is the stairway that crisscrosses the interior courtyard, thus leading to the rooms that are located on several levels. Yes, getting to your room can be like a Stairmaster workout. But the rooms are comfortable, even if they are a bit sparse. Save the occasional group of college students in town for the weekend, this is a quiet hotel. Signs are posted everywhere warning guests against being noisy after 10 PM. However, if you've come to Guanajuato to see the sights, you can't beat the location. Several good bars are just doors away, the Plaza de La Paz is right up the street, and all of the major sites of the historic center are within quick walking distance.

Farther west, at the edge of the colonial center of town, you will come upon a large park called Jardín el Cantador. It is

Mesón del Rosario.

enclosed with a wrought-iron fence and pink stone columns, and is filled with grassy gardens crisscrossed by a series of walking paths leading to the center of the park. This is a strolling park, good for when you want a few quiet moments outside the crowded city. Across the street from this park is the **Mansion** del Cantador (473-732-6888; www.mansiondelcantador.com). This hotel is not far from the Mercado Hidalgo and the Museo de Alhóndiga, and most of the town's other attractions are within walking distance, though the walk to the city center is a bit brisk. It offers 40 rooms and 2 junior suites colorfully decorated in a Mexican art deco style. The hotel also offers a small conference room that has a 40-person capacity and is fully equipped with audiovisual equipment. The on-site Balcones del Cantador restaurant offers up traditional Mexican food; it is open daily from 7:30 AM to 9 PM. Breakfast at the restaurant is included in the room rate for each night's stay. If you are making reservations, keep in mind that this hotel will accept only bank deposits for the first night's payment.

CARRETERA PANORÁMICA

Guanajuato's historic center is built into a steep valley and the Carretera Panorámica, or Panoramic Highway, snakes around the valley rim on almost all sides. This winding road begins in the north, where it crosses Highway 110 (which will take you to Dolores Hidalgo). Not far from where these two highways cross, you will find Hotel La Abadia (473-734-1079; www.hoteleslaabadia.com). This is a very attractive hotel, particularly for its size. With 176 rooms and three restaurants, La Abadia manages to maintain a Mexican boutique look and feel while providing all the amenities of a modern hotel. As with most

hotels in Guanajuato, you should be prepared to walk up a lot of stairs. It features a disco with a full bar, a swimming pool, and several banquet halls that can accommodate up to two hundred people. Room service is also available. The hotel provides transportation service or you can take a taxi downtown. The rooms here are not luxurious, but they are comfortable. Standard rooms are carpeted and are furnished with two double beds. There are also two suites and a small villa available.

Just up the road to the north, you will find another unique hotel that is hard to miss. The hotel Castillo de Santa Cecilia (473-732-0485) occupies an imposing medieval-style castle constructed in the 17th century, and has been a hotel since 1939. However, its interior is much more warm and inviting than the exterior appearance. It offers 66 standard rooms, 15 junior suites, and 7 master suites. Rooms are decorated in an Old World style with stone walls and wrought-iron beds, and generally have very good views of the city. They are furnished with either a king-sized bed or two double beds (master suites have a combination of the two sizes). All suites have separate sitting rooms. Rates for suites here tend to be quite a bit more than for standard rooms and can vary greatly by season. The property features a heated outdoor swimming pool as well as expansive lawns and gardens—and the remnants of a 17th-century silver mine. La Cava restaurant is located here, serving up traditional Mexican cuisine and providing room service. It is open daily from 7 AM to 10 PM. Communication can be a problem here if you don't speak Spanish.

Far to the south along the Carretera Panorámica, on a hill above the center of Guanajuato, you will find the **Hotel Paseo de la Presa** (473-731-0775; www .hotelpaseodelapresa.net). This 58-room hotel looks a bit like a giant green Mexican hacienda that has somehow outgrown itself. Rooms are furnished with two double beds and are decorated in standard hotel room décor, with factory furniture and a small TV sitting on the dresser. Standard room rates are inexpensive and are set for double occupancy; there is an additional charge for each additional occupant. Junior suites are also available. Its La Cascada restaurant offers a nice view of the hotel grounds and serves mostly traditional Mexican food. In the lobby, you will find the El Jardin Bar, which is a nice place to relax and have a drink. The hotel

does have an attractive pool area as well as tennis courts, and several large rooms for banquets and special events with the capacity to serve groups of between 10 and 300 people.

As the Carretera Panorámica snakes still farther south, you will come upon the elegant **Quinta Las Acacias** (473-731-1517; www.quintalasacacias .com). This boutique hotel is in a restored 19th-century French-style mansion right off Florencio Antillón Park. It is filled with European-style furniture and a combination of French and Mexican sensibilities. It is definitely at least worth a walk through. It offers seven rooms and three suites, each one individually decorated with a distinctly European flair. The décor is sure to please anyone who appreciates antiques. The gorgeous restaurant space takes you back a century, serving meals from their international menu daily from 7:30 AM to 11 PM. If you need an excuse to pass the time in interesting surroundings, the hotel also has an attractive sitting room that provides an elegant atmosphere, as well as several terraces—including one with a Jacuzzi.

Also in this part of town, you will find the **Villa Maria Cristina** (473-731-2182; www.villamaria cristina.com.mx/guanajuato).

The pool at Hotel Paseo de la Presa.

Located in a 19th-century neo-classical townhouse, this beautiful boutique hotel offers 13 suites designed for privacy and comfort. They feature high ceilings, wood floors, dark wood furniture, and marble bathrooms with whirlpool tubs. The hotel has a Roman-style spa with a large sunken pool and several treatment rooms where you can be pampered with various treatments and facials. If that doesn't provide enough relaxation, try out the Swiss shower and steam bath, or work out in the on-site gym. There is also a terrace with a large Jacuzzi that is a great place for kicking back and taking it all in. For dinner, try the gourmet cuisine and fine wines found at the on-site restaurant. The hotel also provides private limousine service to the airport in León or even as far away as Mexico City.

For another stylish boutique hotel, follow the Carretera

Panorámica farther still as it turns northwest, where you will find the Casa Colorada (473-734-1151; www.hotelesmision .com). This elegant hotel was built in the 1970s as a center for economic and social studies but in the 1980s was converted into the private retreat of a former Mexican president. In 2002, it was converted into the elegant boutique hotel it is today. It features six tastefully decorated suites with panoramic views of the city below. The Casa Colorada restaurant serves gourmet haute cuisine and fine wines, and also provides a wonderful view of the city. For business meetings and other social events, the hotel has two executive suites with a capacity for 10 to 20 people, audiovisual equipment, wireless Internet access, and meal service.

FARTHER AFIELD

As you get farther away from Guanajuato's historic center, you will find several larger hotels that offer all the amenities that you would expect to find in any decent hotel north of the border, without so much of the colonial ambiance (not to mention the convenience of a good location). One such hotel is the Real de Minas Guanajuato (473-732-1460; www.hotelesrealdeminas

Quick tip: Even if your Spanish is incredibly poor, Mexicans greatly appreciate any effort that you make to speak the language. A quick *"Buenas dias"* will go a long way to earn you respect in the eyes of local residents.

.com.mx). This large hotel features 135 regular rooms and 25 suites. Rooms are relatively spacious and have a fairly interesting décor for this type of hotel. They have carpeted floors with air-conditioning and modern Mexican furnishings. Suites are equipped with Jacuzzi bathtubs. The hotel grounds have a terrace bar, a ladies bar, and a small pool area. The hotel also has 10 conference halls for special occasions of all sizes. The big drawback is that to get to Guanajuato's main attractions, you'll have to hire a taxi.

Another hotel in this area is the Hotel Gran Plaza (473-733-1990; www.hotelgranplaza.com). Located just northeast of the historic center, it offers 107 air-conditioned rooms. Most are furnished with two doubles, though there are a few with one king-sized bed. Rooms are generally what you'd expect to find at a decent chain hotel north of the border. They are simply decorated in a generic style, but comfortable. This hotel has facilities that would make it an option for anyone planning a large event such as a wedding or a reunion. Its La Hacienda restaurant is open from 7 AM to 11 PM serving a variety of local dishes as well as several favorites from north of the border. The Cazadores Bar is open from 2 PM to 11 PM. Room service is also available. The hotel also features a resort-style pool that makes a nice place to relax and have a drink.

Local Flavors

Taste of the town . . .
restaurants, bars, cafés, etc.

JARDÍN DE LA UNIÓN

As with everything else in Guanajuato, the city's culinary life seems to radiate out from the Jardín de la Unión. In the square's southeast corner, you will find El Café Galería (473-732-2566) in a small cubbyhole of a space across the street from Teatro Juárez. However, most of their business takes place at the outdoor tables set up just to the left of the theater's steps. This area is a popular place for foreigners to congregate and have a coffee or a drink. Tables can be hard to get here in the early evening. The menu includes several choices that are more common north of the border, such as hamburgers and french fries. However, there are also plenty of local choices such as enchiladas *mineras* and chicken mole. The food is good but the main attraction is the location, which has a lot of foot traffic and is right next to where street performers often set up to entertain crowds.

If you're looking for a more lively dining experience, head back across the plaza past Teatro Juárez and the Templo San Diego to La Botellita (473-732-7424). This colorful cantina-grill is a fun place to hang out in a TGI Friday's sort of way. To be fair, the décor here is very eye-catching and interesting, creating a stylish feel. Inside you will find a large bar and several rooms of tables with plenty of space for larger parties, unless it's already packed. Located right at the entrance of the Jardín de la Unión, window seats provide great opportunities for people watching. The menu here offers all types of drinks as well as appetizers and full entrees, including a large selection of the

Jardín de la Unión in the evening.

type of Mexican food that any gringo will be right at home with. There are also happy hour specials daily from 3 PM until 7 PM. During festivals and busy weekends this place fills to the rafters and you may have a hard time getting in.

For flavors of Italy, just cross the street to the second floor of the Hotel San Diego. Here, Frascati (473-732-2158) offers a modern décor with an upscale feel. However, the 1980s rock ballads playing low over the sound system didn't add to this ambiance. If you can, get a window seat, with included cool breezes as you look out over the main plaza. The menu offers plenty of Italian favorites, such as lasagna, cannelloni, and shrimp linguini as well as hand-tossed pizzas. There is also complimentary fresh bread and a nice wine list to complement the meal. And if you're not full at the end of your meal, you might consider trying the giant ice cream brownie dessert, which is practically a meal in itself.

*If you like this . . . if you're in the mood for Italian and want a great view of the city, try **El Gallo Pitagorico** (473-732-6758). To get there, walk south behind the Templo San Diego and follow the steep hill up to the right of Bar Ocho and, at the restaurant sign, follow an even steeper set of stairs to this* *hidden Italian restaurant. Just be careful if you walk these steps in the dark. The restaurant is decorated with plenty of Mexican handicrafts, but the menu offers a nice array of Italian specialties such as lasagna and penne* arrabiata. *There are also seafood and steak dishes as well as a large selection of wines and liquors. Getting here can be a chore, but the payoff is equally rewarding. Reservations are recommended.*

If you'd rather be in the middle of the action, instead of viewing it from above, try Restaurante Conde Rul (473-732-9725) at the Hotel Luna.

This restaurant is located right on the Jardín de la Unión, making it an ideal place to meet up with friends. It offers both outdoor seating on the plaza as well as indoor seating in a comfortable dining room. However, keep in mind that—no matter where you sit—the noise can be quite intense at night when the crowds are large and the mariachis are playing. The menu offers primarily Mexican dishes such as enchiladas and chicken mole. However, there are several international dishes on the menu as well, such as spaghetti

Guanajuato at night.

and steaks. This restaurant also offers a good breakfast menu and the Jardín de la Unión is a lovely place to start your day.

A more casual dining experience is available at the northern tip of the square just down from the college bookstore. Good for a quick lunch and e-mail check, the **Café Atrio** (473-731-1213) is an informal place with several lounge chairs as well as several small tables. In the morning, it's a bit like a college cafeteria with bagels, coffee, and juices. For lunch, they offer pastas, salads, tacos, nachos, and even buffalo wings—as well as daily specials of such dishes as enchiladas and mole poblano. From Monday through Thursday, they offer complimentary coffee with the purchase of a slice of pie. Later in the evening, this restaurant transforms into a cocktail bar with jazz and lounge music.

Afterward, satisfy your sweet tooth by visiting **Neveria y Mescelanea Siglo XXI** (473-732-3895), an ice cream shop on the eastern side of the square. There may be no better way to spend an afternoon in Guanajuato than sitting on the benches in this plaza with an ice cream in your hand, watching all the people walk by.

Café Atria.

Fresh-squeezed orange juice is a great way to start your day.

PLAZUELA BARATILLO

For something a bit more upscale, try **El Abue Restaurante** (473-732-6242; www.elabue.com). Located in an attractive house right off the beautiful Plazuela Baratillo, this Mexican-Italian fusion restaurant offers one of the best dining experiences in Guanajuato. The owners have developed recipes from those of their grandparents—who were from Italy and the Oaxacan region of Mexico. The mood is set with quiet music and good service. Dishes are made with quality ingredients and careful attention is paid to presentation here, creating a wonderful dining experience. The atmosphere is elegant but not stuffy. The margaritas are very good, as are the salads. There are continental favorites on the menu, such as filet mignon, as well as Italian and Mexican classics such as lasagna and *chiles en nogada.* Among the surprisingly delicious specialties you will find here are enchiladas *el abue*, dried fruit and meat rolled in tortillas and topped with a red Oaxacan mole sauce. The menu also includes several pasta selections, including fettuccine poblano. The pastas and breads are made daily here. If you're not full, top your whole meal off with apple pie a la mode. Also, if you're looking for a bargain, come for the *menu del día* lunch during the week.

If you like this . . . consider trying Las Mercedes (473-733-9059) off the Carretera Panorámica on the southeast side of town. This elegant Mexican restaurant is located in a house in the hills overlooking Guanajuato. The dining area is impeccably decorated and furnished in a colonial style that is both comfortable and sophisticated. The house is lit with small lamps and fixtures that hang from a wood-beamed ceiling. The walls are covered with paintings and artesenia *knickknacks. The dining experience is further complemented by the view, which overlooks the city. The menu is filled with traditional Mexican favorites such as chicken mole and enchiladas that are beautifully presented. Reservations are highly recommended.*

EAST OF JARDÍN DE LA UNIÓN

Walk down Calle Sopeña away from the plaza to the southeast for about 0.5 block and you will come upon a gem of a restaurant in a 17th-century building that was originally used to melt gold and silver. La Capellina (473-732-9502; www.lacapellina.com) is a simply decorated restaurant offering up an array of interesting dishes. The cuisine here offers a nice mix of Mexican, Italian, Moroccan, and even Thai influences. The menu includes soups, salads, pastas, seafood, meats, and vegetarian dishes. These items range from handmade pizza to salmon with *guajillo* chile to beef filet prepared in red wine. And speaking of wine, there is a nice wine list to complement your meal as well. Come here on the weekends to enjoy bossa nova and Cuban music as well as Latin jazz.

If you get a hankering for coffee or an egg sandwich, walk farther on and between the Museo Iconográfico del Quijote and the Templo San Francisco you will find the Bagel Cafetín (473-733-9733; www.bagelcafetin.com). Decorated with modern art deco furniture, it looks more like a late night drinking lounge but it's actually a great place to stop and get a bagel sandwich. They offer all your favorite espresso and coffee drinks, including frappucinos, as well as juices and Italian sodas. Because the Spanish school Escuela Mexicana is just up the street, you are bound to run into international language students here, making it a great place to meet people. This shop is also equipped with free wireless Internet access, so if you happen to have a laptop on you, this is an excellent place to come and catch up on your e-mail. Just ask at the cash register for the login code.

Plaza de la Paz.

PLAZA DE LA PAZ

To the northwest of Jardín de la Unión, up a slight incline along Calle Obregón, you will come to another triangular plaza. This is Plaza de la Paz, and in colonial times it was the principal plaza of Guanajuato. Flanked on one side by the Basilica Colegiata de Nuestra Señora de Guanajuato and lined with outdoor cafés and shops on the other, this was where aristocrats and wealthy silver lords once made their homes. Located in the center of a garden in front of the basilica is the Monumento a la Paz (Monument to the Peace). This bronze and marble statue of a female was sculpted by the artist Jesús Contreras and added to the plaza in 1898. During festivals vendors set up handicraft and food stands here and the plaza fills to capacity—particularly along Obregón, where the crowd creates a bottleneck of people between Plaza de la Paz and Jardín de la Unión. Along this picturesque square, you will find several outdoor cafés. Among them, Tasca de la Paz (473-734-2225) offers a perfect place for taking in the early morning sun on a springtime day or enjoying an afternoon in this historic plaza. Because this is an open square surrounded by colonial buildings with plenty of foot traffic, this is a good place to people watch and get a feel for this beautiful town. The menu is a

Monumento a la Paz.

Did you know?

Guanajuato is known for a dish called enchiladas *mineras,* or "miner's enchiladas." This is a hearty dish that was likely a favorite among miners after a grueling day deep in the earth. Cheese enchiladas in a red sauce piled high with grilled chicken, roasted

carrots, and potatoes in a bed of shredded lettuce—and topped with crumbled *queso fresco* and Mexican sour cream, this dish looks like a complicated jumble of food. However, it's actually a wonderful blend of flavors that can really satisfy an appetite after a day of touring around. You will find it on the menus of just about every Mexican restaurant in town. Give it a try to experience Guanajuato's tastiest tradition.

Enchiladas mineras is a traditional dish in Guanajuato.

mix of Mexican and Spanish cuisine, including all the traditional favorites such as enchiladas *mineras,* steak *milanesa,* paella, and a variety of Spanish tapas. The menu also offers a good selection of wines and beers, making it a good choice to start off an evening.

PLAZUELA SAN FERNANDO

The Pirinola II (473-117-0610) is just up the street in the Plazuela San Fernando. Located in one of the best plazas in the city, Pirinola II also has a very good *menu del día.* To get here, continue west along Avenida Juárez just past Mesón del Rosario and a *casa de cambio.* To the right, you will see a small stairway leading up into yet another plaza. This is the Plazuela San Fernando, a pretty little square that tends to get better the more time you spend there. It is a lively open place surrounded by many outdoor cafés. Because it is more enclosed than either Jardín de la Unión or Plaza de la Paz, it has a very cozy atmosphere. And

Plazuela San Fernando offers many great restaurant choices.

whereas many of the restaurants in Jardín de la Unión could theoretically have one kitchen hidden away serving them all because their menus are so similar, the restaurants of this plaza are much more diverse. The center of this plaza is often used for university events such as cultural exhibits and music concerts. This is a lovely place to relax with a coffee in the morning as you plan the day's itinerary.

At the back of the plaza, you will see the **Bossanova Crêperia Café** (473-733-1423) with several tables with distinctive yellow tablecloths. This rather relaxing open-air café is reminiscent of something you might expect to

Quick tip: If conversation is going to be an important part of your dinner, you might want to opt for a restaurant in the Plazuela San Fernando over the Jardín de la Unión, which can get crowded and loud.

find in a square in Paris. Coincidentally, the specialty here is crêpes. In fact, they serve 50 varieties of crêpes here, as well as some pretty good espresso drinks. The fruit crêpes are very good, but if you're looking for something really decadent, try the chocolate crêpe. If that wasn't enough, this café does more than just crêpes and coffee. The menu also includes salads and pastas as well as fine wines and a selection of beers. There is also indoor seating available and, in fact, the dining room is attractive. However, this is perhaps the most relaxing plaza in Guanajuato, so you might as well enjoy it. All dishes are prepared with fresh ingredients—no cans.

This being a college town, there are plenty of pizza joints to be found in Guanajuato. Now, there's New York pizza (thin and crispy) and Chicago pizza (thick and loaded)—and then there's Mexican pizza. This pizza tends to be thin and doughy with not as much cheese as you are probably used to. I suspect that most pizza connoisseurs will find Mexican pizza disappointing, just as burger connoisseurs will find Mexican burgers rather disgusting. However, with that understood, the pizza at Pizza Piazza (473-731-1213) is not bad, particularly when you consider the inexpensive price. The restaurant is reminiscent of the pizza parlors you might have eaten at as a kid—kind of dark inside with faux wooden booths and hanging Coke light fixtures. There is no seating on the plaza,

Bossanova Creperia Café offers up delicious creations.

but at the back of the restaurant a large wooden door opens onto the plaza. There's also an old jungle gym inside the restaurant that would never meet American safety standards, but the kids will have fun playing on it if you keep an eye on them.

If you're looking for something a bit more interesting than pizza, head across the square to Café El Midi (473-108-0892). This restaurant is owned and run by a woman named Veronique, who was born in the south of France. She left there many years ago, but she has brought the healthy attitude of the Mediterranean to Central Mexico. This is a buffet-style restaurant that has a beautiful salad bar with fresh vegetables and fresh bread. Most items here are vegetarian, but there are some entrées for the meat eaters out there. In addition to salads, they serve a variety of pies, tarts, and other pastries. This restaurant is also well known for its *agua frescas*, which are slightly less sweet than what you generally find hereabouts. Plus, Veronique offers such wonderful combinations as strawberry-guava and lime-cucumber. There are tables on the plaza where you can sit with a salad and enjoy the day.

If you're really hungry, try the *arranchera*, a common dish in Guanajuato.

For strictly Mexican specialties, try Las Leyendas (473-732-3146), which is also located right on the plaza. This restaurant offers outdoor seating with a relaxed atmosphere and a chance to enjoy Guanajuato's beautiful weather. The menu features plenty of chicken and beef dishes as well as *antojitos*—appetizers such as *taquitos, sopes* (kind of a small, thick tostada), quesadillas, and *flautas.* However, perhaps the most popular dish here is the *arranchera mocajete.* This is a *mocajete* (pronounced mocha-HEH-tay, the stone grinding bowl) filled with chicken, chorizo, beans, and *arranchera* steak—and topped with thick slices of *queso fresco* and a *nopal.* Delicious stuff.

ON TO THE ALHÓNDIGA

If you continue along Avenida Juárez west of Plazuela San Fernando, you will find several other famous Guanajuato landmarks. First you will come upon a Roman arch flanked by a series of columns. This is the entrance to Plaza Reforma, which was built on the grounds of an old corral. It was constructed in 1861 by the architect José Noriega to serve as a marketplace for Guanajuato residents. However, the city's population experi-

enced growth in the late 19th century; in 1910, the Mercado Hidalgo opened and most of the city's merchants relocated there. In 1923 the Plaza Reforma was renovated—with gardens, a central fountain, and eucalyptus and cypress trees. In the center of the plaza is a dried-up *cantera* (quarry) stone fountain surrounded by a series of gardens. There are a few quiet outdoor cafés here and it is a popular place for local families to spend

A Roman arch marks the entrance to Plaza Reforma.

a lazy afternoon, but it is not as well maintained as nearby Plazuela San Fernando. Follow the cobblestone path up the northeast side of Plaza Reforma, and you will come to the Plaza San Roque. In this plaza you will find a baroque church of the same name. There is also a stage here for theatrical performances, particularly during the Cerventino Festival.

Farther along, Avenida Juárez veers to the left and comes to a sharp right turn. Across the street, you will find Plazuela de los Ángeles on your right. This plaza is best known for being near the famed Callejón del Beso, but by itself it is a beautiful little square. There are occasionally musical performances or demonstrations of street theater here. It is also a popular gathering place for local students, and you will often find children here playing near the fountain as their parents sit idly by. Around the corner, on Avenida Juárez, you will find **Tic Tic** (473-732-9502). This traditional Mexican restaurant offers a relaxed family atmosphere and all of the traditional favorites. For breakfast, they offer a variety of dishes served up with a Mexican flair. For lunch or dinner, the chicken mole is wonderful, as are the enchiladas *mineras.* However, the specialty

of the house is *pozole verde,* a hominy soup in a tomatillo broth with chunks of pork. Of course, there is an assortment of wines and Mexican beers to complement your meal as well.

For a more elegant dining experience, continue farther west along Avenida Juárez and turn left at Calle Alhóndiga, where you will find **El Jardín de los Milagros** (473-732-9366; www.eljardindelosmilagros.com .mx). Located in a 17th-century hacienda, this restaurant offers visitors a stylish dining experience in a colonial setting. Attractive dining areas are set among gardens with stone walls and white *zapote* trees as well as in a large dining room. The menu is an interesting mix of Spanish, Mexican, and Mediterranean flavors—exemplified in their chief dish, mahi mahi in cilantro sauce with apples and Spanish pistachios. Great attention is paid to the texture, taste, and presentation of the dishes here. They also offer a wide selection of wines to complement these meals. Reservations are highly recommended.

Also along this street, you will find **El Rincón de los Sabores** (473-732-9502). This elegant restaurant uses seafood as a base to create a diverse menu combining traditional Mexican dishes and international flavors. Here you will find seafood with pasta, fresh vegetables, and other fine ingredients that create a fusion of aromas and tastes. There are several dishes that feature meats and poultry as well. Dining is surprisingly informal here, done in an open-air dining area with shade umbrellas and wrought-iron chairs and tables, perfect for enjoying the wonderful weather of Guanajuato.

If you like this . . . try the Restaurante Teresita (473-731-2183) at the Hotel Maria Cristina. This fine dining restaurant combines sophistication with traditional Mexican cuisine. The gourmet menu changes daily and meals are attractively presented on white dishes. The dining area is a room in off-white colors contrasted with dark-stained woods. High ceilings and an elegant fireplace combine to create an ambiance reminiscent of aristocratic colonial times. There is also an intimate wood-paneled bar area offering fine wines, whiskeys, and tequilas. An interesting array of desserts as well as port wines and sherries are the perfect way to round off your culinary experience.

ALONG POSITOS

Calle Positos, the street where you enter and exit the Alhóndiga, is a long, narrow lane that stretches past the Diego Rivera Museum. Farther on (against

traffic), the walkway becomes treacherously tight as it nears the university. Farther still, the street will bring you to Templo de los Hospitales a few blocks from Jardín de la Unión. Along this street you will find several worthy restaurants. At Positos #52, you will find Chao Bella (473-732-6764), a beautifully decorated Italian restaurant located in a house typical of Guanajuato's historic district. Therefore, dining areas are spread out among several small rooms with just a few tables in each, creating an intimate ambiance. The menu features many authentic Italian pasta dishes such as lasagna and fettuccini, as well as salads and pizzas. There is also a good selection of wines and other spirits to complement your meal. If you're in the mood for a great cup of coffee, head for Positos #35, where the street crosses Calle Juan Valle. Here, in a tiny nook of a restaurant, is Café Conquistador (473-734-1358). It may be small but, if you have a nose, you can't miss its wonderful aroma of fresh-roasted coffee beans. Besides espresso drinks and *café Americano* (American-style coffee), this little café offers baguette sandwiches and pastries. You can also buy coffee by the kilo.

To Do

Check out these great attractions and activities . . .

NIGHTLIFE

There are great nightlife spots to be found throughout Guanajuato's historic center. However, Jardín de la Unión is the place where you are sure to find a crowd. You will find some of the biggest traffic jams along the shaded walkway in front of the Luna Bar (473-732-5054). This bar at the Hotel Luna has enclosed patio seating right on Jardín de la Unión. Always a good place for people watching, this bar attracts locals and travelers alike. Often on weekends, mariachi bands will set up shop right off the patio area and sing traditional songs that everyone seems to know but the gringos. Good food combines with a fun atmosphere to make this bar a good place to begin the night. Next door, Van Gogh (473-732-6903) is another fun place to hang out and have some drinks and eats just to get the night rolling. Located on a patio right on the Jardín de la Unión, it's right in the center of the action and always full of people enjoying themselves. The proprietors often put up a large screen TV during big soccer matches, making this corner of the Jardín a gathering place for cheering fans. This bar also features live music every night. Usually the performers hired by Van Gogh take turns per-

Café Conquistador is a great place to grab a cup of joe.

Hanging out on the steps to Teatro Juárez.

forming with the mariachis parked outside of Luna Bar just over the railing. However, sometimes the mariachis don't play nice and they sing over one another, turning both performances into just a lot of noise. But mostly the atmosphere here is fun loving. Follow the stairs to the second floor and you will find the Vicent lounge bar with a beautiful view of the Jardín de la Unión.

Just a few steps east of the square along Calle Obregón is De Wallen (473-732-0655), a fantastic bar with a rustic, cavelike interior. You have to pay attention to find this bar since there is no sign directing you here. The entrance is a stairwell on Obregón, on the side of the Hotel San Diego. Follow your ears. The interior is wonderful, with exposed stone walls and a large arch right in front of the bar, giving you the feel that you're in some medieval tavern. However, they play the contemporary rock music loud here, so it's hardly a place to sit and have a quiet beer. That said, there aren't a lot of bars like this one in town.

If you're looking for a younger crowd, head south behind the Templo San Diego and the Hotel San Diego to Calle Constancia— where you will find Bar Ocho (473-732-7179). Its name, a play on the

Jardín de la Unión is the place to be in the evening.

word *baracho* (which means drunk) tells you that this isn't the place to come for a quiet cocktail. It is a fun bar that is popular with university and international students. It has a small candlelit patio, a pool table, good food, and a welcoming atmosphere. Come, hang out, and maybe by around 3 AM you just might be *baracho* enough to join in singing songs you don't know the words to. If you are more in the mood for dancing, head up the street to the **Guanajuato Grill** (473-732-0285). This two-level disco is the largest club in Guanajuato, located in a colonial building that is typical of the historic center. It is always packed on the weekend with the university crowd as well as with many thirtysomethings. The interior design may be its most impressive feature, seeming at once modern with a traditional sensibility. It plays a variety of music ranging from techno to *norteño* and offers many drink specials. Down the street to the east is another lounge called **Bora Bora Micheladas and Food** (473-732-1269). This bar, located just behind Teatro Juárez, specializes in *micheladas*, a type of drink that mixes beer, juice, and spices in a salted glass. However, they offer a variety of low-alcohol mixed drinks and wine spritzers. There are several cushioned stools placed around low tables where you can kick back and talk about the day's adventures.

Along Calle Allende, at the north end of Jardín de la Unión, is a college hangout called **Alkatraz** (473-732-0870). This bar booms with lively music, making it popular with the young and beautiful set—with an emphasis on the word "young." It's sometimes hard to get used to the fact that the drinking age is 18, but some of the kids here look as though their high school field trip took a wrong detour. That said, the atmosphere here is animated and enjoyable, with all kinds of drink specials. Some of the drinks you will recognize (sex on the beach, tequila sunrise) and some you might not (*michelada,*

Bora Bora Micheladas and Food just south of Jardín de la Unión

Plaza de la Paz in the evening.

vampiro). Located on the north side of the Jardín de la Unión toward the university, window seats also provide good people watching. Right next door is Corondu (473-732-0445). This is a narrow nook of a billiards hall that fills up with students on weekend nights.

There are several more relaxed options located southeast of the Jardín de la Unión along Calle Sopeña. Among these is Puerta del Sol (473-732-8856). This is a low-lit bar with a relaxed atmosphere. Generally speaking, the crowd here is in their mid-20s or older, making this a nice option for couples looking to avoid the university crowds. A classic cantina bar, there are several tables situated around a stage at the front where local musicians play regularly and visiting musicians play scheduled tour dates. Live music events are held every day but Monday. If you continue past the Templo San Francisco and El Campanero Bridge, you will end up at the Plaza Allende. This small plaza fronts Teatro Cervantes and is dominated by towering statues of Don Quixote and Sancho Panza. Usually this space is fairly empty, save for the occasional young couple looking for a quiet spot to hang out. However, during the Cerventino Festival, this is a busy venue for cultural events. Here, you will find Bar Fly (473-732-5719). This bar is popular with travelers and locals alike. The crowd is fairly international, definitely bohemian, and fairly young—though not postpubescent as is the case at some of the other bars in town; occasionally you'll find some funky thirtysomethings hanging out here as well. They play a lot of reggae music and have a rooftop patio that is great for just hanging out. The décor is interesting, with brightly painted walls and surfboards hanging from the ceiling. There is also a stage where they have live music on the weekends.

In the northwest corner of Plaza de la Paz, you will find Capitolio (473-732-0810). This disco is a favorite among locals and tourists

Las Estudiantinas: The Pied Pipers of Guanajuato

Estudiantina performers play to the crowd in front of the Templo de San Diego.

In 1962, a group of enthusiastic university students became interested in *estudiantina,* a type of traditional Spanish minstrel music played by small instrumental groups. They would get together to sing it and, within a year, they had formed Guanajuato's first *estudiantina* group with the backing of the university. They were known as La Estudiantina de la Universidad de Guanajuato, and they made their debut on the town's cobblestone streets on April 13, 1963. Today, Guanajuato has several student minstrel groups that perform on the city's streets serenading and staging sketches. When night falls over the city, the sound of these groups and accompanying laughter echo through the narrow alleys as they lead crowds of people through the town's winding boulevards.

They gather at dusk in front of Templo San Diego. They're easy to spot in their distinctive costumes that mimic the fashions of 17th-century Spain. The costume is usually a black velvet vest with bright yellow piping worn over a shiny black-and-red-striped shirt. Many of them also carry guitars or lutes. To begin, they warm up the crowd with short skits and dancing. At this time, a member of the group will wander through the crowd soliciting onlookers to join the group on a *callejoneada,* or a walking tour of Guanajuato. This will cost a few dollars and you will receive a cup that they repeatedly fill with libations along the way before making a series of rambunctious toasts. It is also fairly common for people just to follow along with the crowd. As the tour begins, the group of *estudiantinas* leads the crowd up stairs and through narrow alleys. It's important to step carefully, particularly since it can be dark. Usually, there is a member of the group whose sole job is to manage the crowd, pointing out hazardous spots and directing traffic. Along the way, they continuously play music and tell jokes. If you don't speak Spanish, much of this will be lost on you—though the happy atmosphere that is created is definitely contagious, no matter what language you speak. The tour usually ends at the Callejón del Beso, where a young boy always seems to be present, ready to recite the legend.

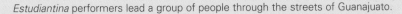

Estudiantina performers lead a group of people through the streets of Guanajuato.

alike. On weekends, this club is always packed with university students. It plays a mix of techno, dance, house, and traditional Mexican music. The club has a large main room in the front and a smaller room in the back that plays principally hip-hop music. The club also has two full bars offering all types of drinks and drink specials. Just south, along Calle Alonso, you will find **Apple** (473-732-6200). This is another bar that is popular with the young local crowd. It plays a lot of electronic music and has a small dance floor. The bar offers plenty of drink specials during the week but not so much on the weekend, when it tends to be crowded. Down the street, **Why Not?** (473-732-2600) is a good option if you're looking for an informal setting. It is a great place to relax and listen to various types of alternative international music such as ska, hip-hop, surfing, reggae, and rock. There are several pool tables here as well.

North of Plaza de la Paz, at the corner of Avenida Juárez and Calle Juan Valle, **B Lounge** (473-732-0662) is a downstairs bar with lots of art deco furniture and bright fluorescent lighting. There are pool tables here and several television screens that play incomprehensible videos, while loud techno music blares in the background. It does seem to be a popular place on some nights, while on others there's not much going on here. Farther up Avenida Juárez, **Las Musas** (473-732-7186) is an intimate upstairs bar located in one of Guanajuato's old houses. It has a very relaxed atmosphere that attracts a bohemian crowd. The drink list is extensive, including many fine whiskeys and tequilas. There is a bar area that's great for hanging out with larger parties. Farther inside, there is a long, narrow stage area filled with tables and chairs. Here is where musicians begin playing mostly acoustic rock music around 7 PM each night. There are windows here that look out onto Avenida Juárez, and you can hear the music down the street.

SHOPPING

If you are in the market for Mexican handicrafts, you can't go wrong in Guanajuato. There are several interesting shops in the Plaza de la Paz and along its environs. For a relaxing day of lazy shopping, stroll along Calle Positos to #64 where you will find **El Viejo Zaguán** (473-732-3971; www.viejozaguan.com), located in an old historic house. With soft music playing in the background, this handsome little store has a selection of books, music, Mexican art, and coffee. Enjoy an

The Plaza de La Paz is lined with many interesting shops.

espresso drink while you peruse their carved Oaxacan *alebríjes* and paintings (and reproductions) by local artists. If you're in need of something to read, head down to Positos #30 (across the street from the Diego Rivera Museum) and Donkey Jote (473-734-0455), the only English language bookstore in Guanajuato.

Although it is Dolores Hidalgo that has become famous as the area's *talavera* center, it is in fact Guanajuato that is home to the area's highest quality workshops. You can visit these workshops yourself to both see the artisans at work and make your purchases directly. Casa de Capelo (473-732-0612) is located 5 km north of town along Highway 110, on the road to Dolores Hidalgo. This is the workshop of the famous Guanajuato ceramist Javier de Jesús Hernández, known simply as Capelo. He is also a painter and a university professor, and he has worked out of this workshop for more than 30 years. Here you will find a small showroom of museum-quality *talavera*. These pieces are made according to Spanish colonial majolica designs guaranteed to meet U.S. standards for lead content. The city's other important *talevera* workshop is Gorky González Quiñones (473-731-0462; www.gorkypottery.com). This is the workshop of the world-renowned ceramist known simply as Gorky. This workshop is located in the Pastita area east of the city center. They have a large showroom with all manner of ceramic artwork. If you make an appointment, you can also tour the workshop during the week to see the pieces being made. Like Capelo, the pieces here are produced according to the majolica design standards of the Spanish colonial period (and they meet U.S. lead content standards as well). These two artists are the only ceramists in Mexico still working by these techniques.

Mercado Hidalgo

Along Avenida Juárez across the street from the Church of Belén you will find Mercado Hidalgo, the city's primary market. This market was built at the beginning of the 20th century on the site of an old bullfighting ring, and was inaugurated in 1910 by President Porfirio Diaz. It has a pink *cantera* stone neoclassical façade—though, from the inside, it looks more like a converted aircraft hangar. The building is about 75 yards long and has three entrances.

It is said that this building was originally meant to be a train station. However, when it was finished, the main marketplace that was formerly located at Plaza Reforma was moved here. The ground floor of the market is filled largely with vendors selling produce, meats, and candies; there are also food stalls located here. Around the upper periphery and scattered throughout the ground floor are merchants selling clothing, crafts, and souvenirs. However, don't expect a shopping mall when you come here. This is a chaotic and cramped place where you can find cheap toys and gifts, and where you may see vendors selling odd items such as knockoff DVDs and dog-eared pornographic magazines. It's certainly not the most pleasant place in Guanajuato, but it is interesting. If you do find something you like, don't be afraid to barter for it.

Practice your bartering skills at Mercado Hidalgo.

Guanajuato is a city that is revered throughout Mexico for its beauty and cultural importance. Groups of schoolchildren commonly wander its streets on cultural field trips from nearby towns, gazing up at El Pípila towering above the city, and lunching on the steps of the square in front of the Alhóndiga Museum. The thing that is striking about this relatively small colonial city is the dense wealth of impressive churches, plazas, museums, and colonial architecture. However, it's only when you begin to dig deeper, by learning the stories behind the city's beauty, that you really begin to appreciate Guanajuato. From the heroic bravery behind El Pípila to the tragic love of Callejón del Beso, this city will never cease to grab your interest and amaze you.

On the west side of colonial Guanjuato, at a narrow alley where two balconies hang just 27 inches apart, is the Callejón del Beso—"alley of the kiss." It has become famous for a tragic incident that supposedly occurred here. Legend has it that the home on the left (viewed from the alley entrance) was once home to Doña Carmen, the only daughter of a violent and obstinate man. After discovering her being courted at church by a young man by the name of Don Luis, Carmen's father locked her in her room. He had plans to marry her off to a rich man in Spain in order to restore his dwindling fortune. Hearing this news, Luis became desperate to see his love and purchased the home across the alley—knowing that the window in her home gave onto the balcony, where he could get close enough to touch her. One night, as the two sweethearts stood at the balconies holding hands, Carmen's father burst into the room and plunged a dagger into her heart. Stunned, Luis could

El Campanero Bridge.

A couple poses at Callejón del Beso.

only place a kiss on Carmen's lifeless hand before letting go. Okay, it's a depressing story without the subtlety and grandeur of a Shakespearean sonnet, but it's still worth a look. To get here, go to Plazuela de los Ángeles off Avenida Juárez, and walk about 50 yards up Callejón del Patrocinio on the right side of the plaza. Callejón del Beso is on the left. There is no charge to enter but this is a popular spot, so you may have to wait several minutes to get in.

On the other side of town, between the Museo Iconográfico del Quixote and Teatro Cervantes, **El Campanero Bridge** is a short, picturesque *cantera* stone bridge built in 1778 to provide street access to a house on Subida del Tecolote that belonged to a wealthy resident. The house originally had its entrance on the street level. However, because the street was lowered on two separate occasions to allow carriages to pass through, the bridge became necessary. The house itself also had to be modified; a window was converted into the primary entrance, and stairs were added in the foyer of the house next door. The name *El Campanero,* or "bell ringer," comes from the fact that men would stand on this bridge in the 19th century and ring a bell to announce the arrival and departure of carriages. Today, the bridge is used as the patio for the Santo Café.

High above the town is the towering rose-colored monument known as **El Pípila**. As the story goes, José de los Reyes Martínez—who went by the nickname of *El Pípila*—was a native of San Miguel de Allende working in the mines of Guanajuato in September of 1810, when Miguel Hidalgo arrived with his band of insurgents. *El Pípila* quickly took up with Hidalgo, whose goal in Guanajuato was to take the Granaditas Corn Exchange (the present-day site of the Alhóndiga del Granaditas Museum). Guanajuato's provincial governor, Juan Antonio de Riaño y Barcena, had taken up position in this building

El Pípila.

A tram offers the easiest way to get to El Pípila.

with the soldiers of the garrison; they guarded a treasure of some 3 million pesos in silver ingots and cash from the Royal Tax Office, as well as military equipment and food supplies. A bloody battle ensued in which *El Pípila* put a large piece of flagstone on his back to protect him from the Spanish gunfire and crawled to the door of the corn exchange with a torch in his hand. He set fire to the door, eventually allowing the insurgents to take the building. This monument was erected in 1939 to honor José de los Reyes Martínez's bravery and commitment to Mexican independence. The statue is in a plaza paved with cobblestones and ringed by a balustrade, and there is a door to a staircase at the back of the monument which takes you to the top. Besides being an amazing statue, there are stone bleachers at its feet that face out toward the city and provide a spectacular panoramic view day and night of Jardín de la Unión and the rest of this colorful town. To get here, walk south on Calle Sopeña from Jardín de la Unión and turn right up Callejón del Calvario. Follow the signs to El Pípila. The monument is about a ten-minute walk uphill along this alley and along Subida de San Miguel, so be sure to wear comfortable shoes. If the walk is too brisk for you, hop on a city bus marked EL PÍPILA. The ride will cost three pesos, or about a quarter.

As you stand under El Pípila and gaze out over the city, one of the many edifices that will strike you is a long white stairway that rises elegantly just beyond the basilica. This is the Universidad Autónimo de Guanajuato. This site was first developed as a hospice by Jesuit missionaries with the help of Doña Josefa Teresa de Busto y Moya, the wife of a wealthy mine owner. She and several of her wealthy friends donated the money to establish the first school in what was then a sleepy mining village. In 1744, the Spanish crown granted the Jesuits in Guanajuato a license to operate their hospice as a college. They called it the College of the Holy Trinity and offered courses in arts and letters. The Jesuits began construction of the Church of La Compañía de Jesús in 1747—and the adjacent building, which would eventually house the college as it exists today, began construction in 1759. However, the Jesuits were expelled from New Spain eight years later due to political conflict between the Spanish crown and the papacy in Rome. As a result, the college remained unfinished—with only one floor having been built. Later, in 1796, a new boarding college was established on the site; offering courses in art, rhetoric, and philosophy, it continued to operate throughout the turbulent years of the fight for Mexican independence. In 1828, the state government took ownership of the college and turned it into a public institution by the name of the College of the Immaculate Conception, offering courses in mining and law. In 1867, after many chaotic years, the name changed once again to the National College of Guanajuato. However, it wasn't until 1945, when it gained university status, that the current institution was born. It was at this time that the main building was remodeled and expanded into the grandiose edifice that exists today. This impressive neoclassical building houses the rector's office, administrative and academic offices, as well as a number of the university's schools and faculties. This institution is largely responsible for the vivacious atmosphere that permeates the city of Guanajuato today. Its students are a

Quick tip: The easiest way to get up to El Pípila is to follow the alley on the east side of Teatro Juárez to the tram station on the left. The ride costs a couple of bucks but it's much faster than the bus and a heck of a lot easier than hiking up.

Universidad Autónimo de Guanajuato.

constant complement to the Jardín de la Unión, and they have created a nightlife like no other this side of Mexico City. Students also
make up the bulk of the city's street performers, such as the wandering minstrels and the clowns that entertain daily in front of Teatro
Juárez. To get to the university from Plaza de La Paz, walk north on
Calle de Estudiante from the north side of the basilica. You can also
walk east on Calle Positos, and continue along Lascuráin de Retana
when you cross Calle Juan Valle.

ARTS AND CULTURE

Museums

Guanajuato has many museums that are well worth a visit. And if you
plan on taking the time to enjoy these, you may want to begin with
Calle Positos, where many of these museums are located. Among the
best is Museo de la Alhóndiga de Granaditas (473-734-1062). Looking at this worn, square building, you might not guess that it's actually
one of the most important edifices in this architecturally rich city.
However, when you think about it, the Alhóndiga does wear its history for all to see. Though today it houses great art, this building was
originally built to store grain. In the opening days of the Mexican War
for Independence, however, fate took over. This was the site of a storied battle in which the insurgent forces, led by the now-famous *El
Pípila*, seized this strategically important building. However, a slaugh-
ter ensued afterward—one that convinced many people who were
considering joining the move for independence to remain loyal to
Spain. Later the Spanish forces retook Guanajuato, and in order to
dissuade residents from further insurrection, they hung the heads of
the insurgent leaders Hidalgo, Allende, Aldama, and Jiménez from
the four corners of this building—where they remained for a decade.
Even after that, the Alhóndiga was just about as far away from being
a museum as you could imagine. In 1864, the building was converted
into the state penitentiary of Guanajuato. Finally, in 1949 renovation
began to turn the interior of this neglected neoclassical building into
a regional museum that would display an impressive collection that
spanned the pre-Hispanic era right through the colonial days of Mexico's past. The collection, which is located on the second floor surrounding the interior courtyard, is divided into four major themes.
The first is the ethnographic, which includes an assortment of regional crafts. The second is the archaeological, which comprises more

than five thousand pieces of indigenous artwork from pre-Hispanic Mexico. Prominent pieces among this collection include an assortment of ancient stamping tools. The third section is historical, with objects dealing with Mexico's struggle for independence. Much of this collection was donated by the artists Olga Costa and José Chavez Morado. The final section is a fine art collection with paintings from artists such as Hermenegildo Bustos. However, perhaps the museum's most impressive display is the mural by José Chávez Morado on the walls of the stairway that depicts Mexico's revolutionary wars and folk traditions. Located one block north of the Mercado Hidalgo and two blocks west of the Diego Rivera Museum, the Alhóndiga is probably the major sight farthest from the center of town that still manages to be within walking distance.

Detail from a mural by José Chávez Morado in the Alhóndiga.

Across the street from the Alhóndiga is the **Museo de Cera Guanajuato** (551-395-9107; www.museodeceradeguanajuato .com.mx). This wax museum does not have the historical significance of the Alhóndiga, or indigenous artwork that has been around for hundreds of years. But where else are you going to find a creepy sculpture of Tom Cruise in the next room over from Jesus Christ? This museum does seem to have a little bit for everybody. If you're interested in heroic figures that shaped the history of Mexico, you'll find them in the first room to the right, where the bloody decapitated heads of Hidalgo, Allende, Aldama, and Jiménez sit in bird cages—preserved for eternity exactly as the Spanish displayed them two hundred years ago just across the street at the Alhóndiga. If you're looking for religious figures—yes, you

Quick tip: The Diego Rivera Museum offers weekly cultural events for the whole family. When you arrive in town, head over to the museum to pick up the schedule so you don't miss anything.

can stand in the same room with Jesus and Pope John Paul II. Or if you're just in the mood for inexplicable life-size wax sculptures of movie stars, Tom Cruise and Sean Connery are here for you, too. Rumor has it that Robert de Niro and Bruce Willis are soon to join them. All in all, this museum is fun for a quick excursion—and since it's right across the street from the Alhóndiga, it's not all that far out of the way either. The tour ends with a horror-filled room of zombies and disemboweled wax corpses that might be too much for young children, but mostly it's a good time.

The famous muralist Diego Rivera was born and lived his early life in a large 19th-century neoclassical house along Calle Positos in Guanajuato. Today, this house is the **Museo Casa Diego Rivera** (473-732-1197). Even if this house did not have this distinction, it would

The Diego Rivera Museum offers many events that are free to the public.

A gallery at the Diego Rivera Museum.

be worth the price of admission just to walk through and see how the residents of Guanajuato have laid out their homes on multiple floors. Diego Rivera was a world-renowned painter famous for his leftist views and politically provocative murals, as well as for being the husband of Frida Kahlo. In the early- to mid-20th century, Rivera painted murals in places as remote as San Francisco, Detroit, and New York. Today, his work is displayed in many of the world's most prominent museums. This museum opened in 1975, after several years of restoration. The ground floor of the museum has a small gift shop and showcases the original furniture that belonged to the Rivera family at the end of the 19th century. The upper floors display approximately one hundred works by Rivera, comprising a collection that is considered one of the most important in Mexico. As you make your way to the upper floors, you will see that this wonderful collection of works is representative of the different stages of his artistic career—including a variety of techniques and mediums such as oil paints, pencil, ink, lithography, and watercolor. The museum also presents temporary exhibitions of different works of the plastic arts, as well as cultural events on Tuesday through Sunday from 10 AM to 1:15 PM and from 4 PM to 6:30 PM.

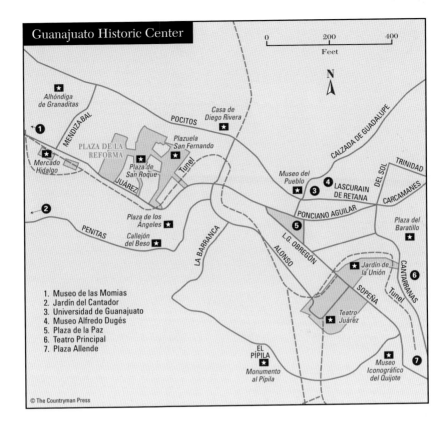

Guanajuato Historic Center

0   200   400
Feet

N

1. Museo de las Momias
2. Jardín del Cantador
3. Universidad de Guanajuato
4. Museo Alfredo Dugés
5. Plaza de la Paz
6. Teatro Principal
7. Plaza Allende

© The Countryman Press

*If you like this . . . spend some time at the **Museo de Arte Olga Costa–José Chavez Morado** (473-731-0977). This museum is located in the 17th-century tower at the Hacienda de Guadalupe. In 1966, a pair of painters—Olga Costa and José Chavez Morado—acquired this estate in order to convert it into a home and studio for Costa. In 1990, the artists opened the tower to the public as a museum that bore both of their names. In 1993, shortly before the death of Costa, they donated the museum (along with the collection within) to the state government of Guanajuato. The collection comprises approximately five hundred pieces, including furniture, works of contemporary art, and original work by the couple.*

Farther east toward the university is the **Museo del Pueblo de Guanajuato** (473-732-2990). This museum houses a collection of 18th- and 19th-century art donated to the people of Guanajuato in 1979 by the artists José Chavez Morado and Olga Costa. The museum also holds temporary exhibitions. It is located in a 17th-century building with a churrigueresque chapel built in 1776 that serves as the Olga Costa Auditorium, decorated with murals and furniture that

A display of miniature artwork at the Museo del Pueblo de Guanajuato.

was once owned by Morado himself. Unfortunately, this chapel was defaced, probably sometime during the 19th century.

In the main building on the campus of the University of Guanajuato is the **Alfredo Dugés Natural History Museum** (473-732-0096). It was founded in December 1941 in honor of Alfredo Dugés, a French scientist who was a professor here during the years it was a state college in the 19th century. Dugés specialized in amphibians and reptiles, but this collection exhibits a wide variety of samples of local plants, animals, and fossils. It also houses a collection of watercolors and drawings of flora and fauna made by Dugés during his study of the region. Also on the campus, at the Faculty of Mining, is the Museo de Mineralogía (473-732-2291). It features nearly twenty-five thousand examples of minerals from all over the world, all identified in Spanish. However, if you can remember your chemical formulas, you should be okay. Most are encased in glass, though several larger specimens (such as a giant geode) are out in the open. It's not for everybody, but if you're a fan of geology, this might be an interesting place to spend an hour or two.

Several blocks to the south, you will find the Museo Iconográfico del Quijote (473-732-3376; www.museoiconografico.guanajuato.gob .mx). This museum demonstrates why the UNESCO Center of Castilla–La Mancha in Spain conferred upon the city of Guanajuato the title of Cervantine Capital of the Americas during the 400-year anniversary celebration of the novel *Don Quixote de la Mancha*. The museum came to fruition thanks to the donation of Eulalio Ferrer, a Spanish refugee and Quixote enthusiast who adopted Mexico as his second home country. The museum was inaugurated in 1987 in a

A family passes the day enjoying artwork at the Museo del Pueblo de Guanajuato.

ceremony that marked the fifteenth Cervantes Festival. In attendance was the Mexican president, Miguel de la Madrid, as well as the prime minister of Spain, Felipe Gonzalez. It contains an extensive collection of paintings, sculptures, drawings, tapestries, and other artwork dedicated to Don Quixote—the sad, chivalrous figure—and his loyal squire Sancho Panza, characters created by Miguel de Cervantes in what is considered the world's first novel. Some of the works of art are true masterpieces, including pieces by Mario Orózco Rivera, Salvador Dali, and Pablo Picasso.

If you like this . . . make sure you pay a visit to Plaza Allende, where you will find a giant statue of Don Quixote and his sidekick, Sancho Panza.

Statue at the entrance of Museo Iconográfico del Quijote.

Perhaps the most famous museum in Guanajuato is the Museo de las Momias (473-732-0639; www.momiasdeguanajuato.gob.mx/english/index.html). Mexicans have a running joke in which they will tell you they have a relative in Guanajuato. The punch line comes when they tell you that this relative resides at the Museo de las Momias. This museum is widely regarded as one of Guanajuato's biggest attractions. In fact, anyone who knows Guanajuato will likely ask you if you visited. However, the exhibits at this macabre museum are not likely to satisfy anyone's anthropological interests—being that the bodies on display here are not mummies at all, but are instead just a collection of unfortunate corpses. What you are likely to bring away from this place is a deeper appreciation of the cultural differences in the way with which Mexicans deal with death—and quite possibly you will leave feeling a little sick. The mummy museum displays 119 bodies exhumed during the years that the grave tax was enforced. Perhaps their most interesting aspect is their tattered clothing, some of which dates to the late 19th century. Other than this minor fascination, this museum seems to have the effect of making visitors ponder their own fates. The drying process has contorted the faces of these poor people so that they all seem to be frozen in a permanent state of agony. Sadly, several of the subjects have not only met an unpeaceful end, but an undignified one as well. Clumps of matted hair cling to exposed skulls, toes poke through deteriorated boots, and torn clothing reveals dehydrated genitals. However, perhaps the museum's most disturbing exhibit is its finale: a mother and child who both died in the act of childbirth. The woman still displays the long scar from the attempted cesarean section and the emaciated child is propped upright and labeled *LA MOMIA MÁS PEQUEÑA DEL MUNDO* (The smallest mummy in the world). Needless to say, this museum is not for everybody. And when asked if you visited it, you can always say you lost track of time over at Diego Rivera's house instead.

Many tours that take you to the mummy museum will also stop at the Valenciana Mine. At one time this mine was by far the most important silver mine in the world, producing fully ⅔ of the silver that packed Spanish coffers during the colonial period. It was discovered in 1548 and reached its production peak in 1760, when miner Antonio de Ordoñez unearthed a silver deposit of incalculable value.

Some of the gruesome faces to be seen at the Mummy Museum.

Did you know?

Between the late 19th century and the 1950s, local law required relatives of deceased persons to pay a grave tax. If the family failed to pay the tax, the body was exhumed. It was quickly discovered that the mineral-rich earth and dry climate of the area seemed to mummify anything buried in it. In the early 1900s, these strangely preserved bodies began attracting tourists, cemetery workers quickly discovered that they could charge people viewing fees—and the museum was established. However, interest in this gruesome spectacle really took off in 1970 with the release of the popular movie *Santo Versus the Mummies of Guanajuato*, which starred the masked wrestler Rodolfo Guzmán Huerta.

The mine continues to be in operation today, with a main tunnel that is more than 1,700 feet deep. There are two nearby shafts—El Nopál and San Ramón—that are used as show mines for tourists. These tours have trained guides and accident insurance. The tour of the Valenciana Mine takes you through a series of rooms in an old building filled with artifacts that tell the history of the mine. Displays of old black-and-white photos show the owners and workers that have lived and died here over the years—and many did die. In fact, a miner's life expectancy was about 10 years from the first time he stepped foot in the mine. Needless to say, the miners working here—made up mostly of young indigenous men—were savagely exploited. You learn what it was all for in the final room, where you will find a series of cases filled with gleaming silver plates, pitchers, and jewelry made from that shiny metal dug out of the earth below. At this point of the tour,

Inside the Valenciana Mine.

A guide demonstrates torture techniques at Museo Ex-Hacienda del Cochero.

you begin a descent into the narrow mineshaft. As you walk down the twisting stairwell, it is hard to imagine how workers managed to get their equipment down to where they would need it.

Another macabre experience can be found north of town at the Museo Ex-Hacienda del Cochero (473-733-4766). This museum was once the site of Inquisition-style tortures. Today you can get a tour of the hacienda's dungeon, which is filled with all sorts of implements of torture. Unfortunately, the tour is entirely in Spanish; however, there is plenty here of interest even if you don't understand the tour guide. The items are almost unbelievable in their cruelty, and the fact that they were once actually used on human beings is a very sobering thought.

Another museum located outside of town that is well worth a visit is the Museo Ex-Hacienda San Gabriel de Barrera (473-732-0619). In the late 17th century, Captain Gabriel de la Barrera became a wealthy mine owner and established a series of haciendas and ore-concentrating mills throughout the area that carried his name—including Hacienda de Barrera Grande, Hacienda de Barrera en

Medio, Hacienda de San Antonio de Barrera, Hacienda de Dolores, and Hacienda de Sacramento. This hacienda, originally known as Hacienda de Barrera Grande, was without a doubt the most important in the area—as well as one of the most beautiful. After many changes in ownership throughout the centuries, it was acquired by the Guanajuato state government in the mid-1970s, and opened to the public as a museum in 1979. It offers visitors the chance to stroll along its beautiful grounds and get a sense of what life on a Mexican hacienda was really like. This 237,000-square-foot estate is divided into three parts. The first is the main house, which contains the museum offices and many impressive rooms filled with 18th-century paintings, furniture, and tapestries. The second part is a small chapel featuring a 15th-century Spanish altarpiece where the Barreras' personal religious services were held. The third and final section is a work area that features the location where the precious ore was extracted—now converted into 17 unique gardens, including courtyards that are wonderful for relaxing in while enjoying a beautiful day. Here you will also find the storage rooms, aqueducts, waterwheels, tanks, and horse stables that housed the horses necessary for mining silver ore.

Theater

Crowning the center of town, **Teatro Juárez** (473-732-1542) is considered one of the most beautiful theaters in Mexico. Inaugurated in 1903 by President Porfirio Diaz, it has a neoclassical façade crowned by bronze statues of the Greek muses. The wide steps of the theater are flanked by two bronze lions and a *cantera* balustrade leading to a series of fluted Doric columns of green *cantera* stone. Inside the theater, a Moorish-influenced lobby leads to five levels of seating that open to the auditorium—decorated throughout with intricate arabesque detail, and with a curtain adorned with a painting of Constantinople. It is reputed to be the only theater in Mexico that has conserved its original furnishings. This theater presents plays, ballet, and lectures, among other cultural activities.

Behind the north side of Jardín de la Unión is **Teatro Principal** (473-732-1523). This theater was originally built at the height of Guanajuato's mining heyday in 1788, to give the city a bit of culture. For more than a century it remained the town's only theater, and over its more than two hundred years it has had a rich but tumultuous history. It has entertained common people and prominent figures alike, and it

Teatro Juárez sits at the center of Guanajuato.

has been abandoned and subsequently restored several times. In 1921, after being converted to a commercial cinema, it burned down. In 1955, it was rebuilt and has since been run by the Universidad de Guanajuato—all the while enjoying a successful cultural scene of theater, ballet, lectures, and other activities.

Several blocks southeast of Teatro Juárez, in Plaza Allende, is Teatro Cervantes (473-732-1169). This theater is a neoclassical building similar to the construction of the Alhóndiga. It has two floors and a capacity of 430 people. In 1979, it was converted into a theater for the Cerventino Festival, with large statues of Don Quixote and his trusted squire Sancho just outside. This theater is mainly used for cultural events during the Cerventino Festival.

Sacred Sites

The Basilica Colegiata de Nuestra Señora de Guanajuato sits in the heart of Guanajuato and is the main backdrop of the Plaza de la Paz. Even from El Pípila, this edifice stands out among the town's many architectural wonders. Many authorities consider the façade of this church to be the purest example of baroque architecture in Mexico.

Teatro Cervantes is a good example of neoclassical construction.

Basilica Colegiata de Nuestra Señora de Guanajuato dominates the Plaza de la Paz.

Between 1691 and 1696, it was built (with funds from lucrative nearby mines) to be the town's parish church. The Templo de los Hospitales was previously the primary parish church in town. The basilica is laid out in a Latin cross configuration that is nearly 200 feet long and nearly 30 feet wide. Amazingly, it is nearly 50 feet high in the vault and almost 100 feet high in the central dome— making it the largest building in the city. It consists of two bell towers, a very large one on the north side and a smaller one on the south, with a clock that was added in the late 18th century. In 1957, this parish church rose to the rank of basilica.

Did you know?

Every region of Mexico has its own particular brand of *baile folk-lórico*. Even the costumes are specific to each region, though they are always flamboyant outfits for the men and beautifully flowing, brightly colored dresses for the women—who also wear ribbons intricately woven into their hair. *Baile folklórico* dancers spend years learning the nuances of their region's distinct style of dance, often beginning early in their childhood. Performers create their interpretations through specific body positions, group formation, music, and scenery.

Baile folklórico dancers.

The church houses several early artifacts, including the much-revered statue of the Virgin of Guanajuato, a carved wooden figure on a silver base that is believed to date back to the 7th century. This statue was presented to the city by King Philip II of Spain in 1557. In fact, the need to provide a suitable home for this statue is partly what prompted the town to build this church.

This church has three entryways. Each doorway has an intricate baroque facade of pink stone. The atrium is neoclassical and was built between the 18th and 19th centuries. There is also a neoclassical chapel near the baptistery, a section built in the late 19th century. The Count of Valencia donated the body and blood of Saint Faustina to the basilica in 1826, and these remains were placed in a chapel altar, which was done by the architect Edward Tresguerras. In 1907, to mark the canonical patronage of the Virgin of Guanajuato, the remains of the saint were transferred to the upper altar. Sunday mass here (10 AM and noon) is usually standing room only.

Just down the street, the Templo San Diego de Alcántara occupies the south end of the Jardín de la Unión. It has a churrigueresque

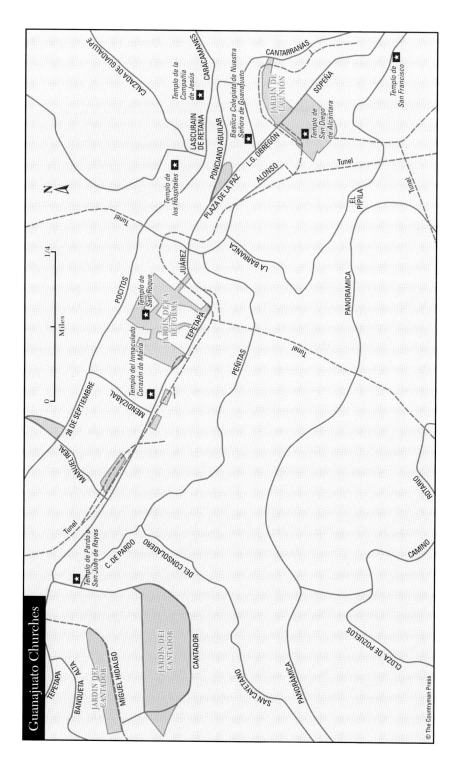

Guanajuato Churches

© The Countryman Press

Did you know?

The first construction of a church on the site of the Templo San Diego began in 1663. It was commissioned by friars of the Franciscan order of Dieguina, also known as the "Barefoot Franciscans." The church cemetery was once located on the site that Teatro Juárez now occupies. Nothing of that original construction exists today, due to destructive floods and reconstructions that took place in 1694 and 1780.

façade of pink quarry stone embedded with intricate carvings. On the inside, you will find two chapels known as the Purísima Concepción and the Chapel of the Señor de Burgos. These chapels contain several 18th-century treasures—including a painting that has survived several floods, and a series of paintings that depict the life of San Pedro de Alcántara, the founder of the order of Dieguina.

A few blocks north, you will find Templo de los Hospitales. In 1565, this church opened as the first church of Guanajuato. It was commissioned by the bishop of Michoacán, Vasco de Quiroga, and doubled as a hospital for the local indigenous population. It is the original parish church of Guanajuato and is known today simply as the Church of the Hospitals. Outside of a few improvements made to the church around 1940, its original interior has survived intact. Although today this church is usually closed, it is a historically and religiously important location for the town since it is the town's original church, as well as the place where the Virgin of Guanajuato statue was displayed for 130 years before the basilica was built in 1696.

Less than a block south of the Museo Iconográfico del Quixote you will find the Templo San Francisco. The entrance to this 18th-century orange baroque church is elevated to protect it against floods; the intricately carved churrigueresque stonework of plant motifs and niches contains images of Saint Peter and Saint Paul. Above it is a circular clock framed with green quarry stone. The façade is finished with bell towers on either side of the entrance, each containing double-level arches topped with small domes. In the interior, you will find images of the Virgin as well as Saint Francis of Assisi adorning the main altar. As with most of the churches

The interior of Templo de los Hospitales is cavernous.

in the city, the original baroque altar has been replaced by a later neoclassical model. On Sunday, masses are held at 10:30 AM.

Right across the street from the Mercado Hidalgo, the baroque exterior of the Templo del Inmaculado Corazón de María (Belén) appears cracked and faded. However, if you are lucky enough to get a look inside, you will find the interior to be imposing and beautiful. Its churrigueresque entrance rises from the ground all the way to the top of the church, containing niches with sculptures of Saint Anthony and Santo Domingo de Guzmán. The central niche is occupied by a statue of the Virgin Mary; this aged façade dates back to the 1770s. The inside of the church is laid out in a Latin cross configuration, with a neoclassical altar dating back to the 19th century. The left side of this altar is devoted to the Virgin of Guadalupe, while on the right side is a large sculpture of the sacred heart of Jesus. The pulpit is renowned for its fine gold work.

In the Plaza San Roque, just off Plazuela San Fernando and Plaza Reforma and not far from the Diego Rivera Museum, is the Templo San Roque. It was constructed in 1726 and is one of the purely neoclassical churches in the region. One of the first things you will notice about it is that, unlike the more intricate churrigueresque churches in town, the façade of this church is sober—with straight lines and almost no decorative carvings. The door of the church is beautifully carved and forms a medium-sized arch flanked by niches with religious statues. Above the door, the façade emphasizes a rectangular choral window flanked by fluted pilasters. Inside, the neoclassical altar has a niche with a statue of the Virgin of the Rosary. However, this church is perhaps best known as the backdrop for the *entremeses*, or short skits, performed in its plaza during the Cerventino Festival. This plaza was chosen as the setting of the first *entremeses* performed in Guanajuato in February of 1953, because it is said to resemble 16th-century Spain.

If you venture to the north side of town, up a series of winding streets toward the Carretera Panorámica, you will come upon the Santuario de Mineral de Cata. During the heyday of the silver boom, it was customary for successful miners to build chapels at the worksites as a way of giving thanks and fulfilling their religious obligations. The baroque church at the Mineral de Cata Mine is one such church. It has an impressive churrigueresque façade flanked by a single tower. It was commissioned by Alonso de Villaseca, a wealthy miner who owned mines throughout the region and had a hacienda nearby. It was actually built to house the statue of Christ you can see inside today. Construction on the church began in 1709 but, because of delays brought about by fluctuations in the mine's production, it wasn't finished until 80 years later. The Santuario de Mineral de Cata is now a destination of religious importance for worshipers through-out Mexico who come here to admire the Christ of Villaseca and ask for God's grace and good favors.

Construction on **Templo de la Compañía de Jesús** began in 1746 and was concluded 20 years later under the direction of the Friar José de la Cruz, a member of the Jesuit Order (Compañía de Jesus). He designed a façade with three churrigueresque doors, and niches for images of Jesuit saints. He was assisted by the Mexican architect Philip of Ureña, who probably only completed the tower. Much of this church is not original. The original dome collapsed in 1808 and, to preserve the church, it largely had to be reconstructed in the late 19th century by the architect Herculaneum Ramirez. The baroque altar-pieces were replaced with neoclassical additions in the 19th century, as was much of the atrium. However, this church contains an impor-tant collection of Miguel Cabrera paintings from the 18th century.

LANGUAGE SCHOOLS

Acadamia Falcon (473-731-0745; www.academiafalcon.com) is locat-ed just outside the center of town, in the neighborhood of La Presa, named after the nearby Presa de la Olla. It occupies the houses and gardens of a former private estate and provides a relaxed learning environment for students. The classroom and dormitory building have nice views of the surrounding mountains. This school breaks the learning of language into four categories: reading, speaking, writing, and listening. With this in mind, they use a variety of teaching meth-ods to hone these skills. Classes start every Monday and the program teaches total immersion Spanish. There is also a kid's program for all levels of learners. If you like, the school will also set you up with a host family. One-on-one classes are also available.

Escuela Mexicana (473-732-5005; www.escuelamexicana.com) is located in a cavernous house just up the street from the Museo Iconográfico del Quixote. They offer classes year-round at all skill lev-els. When you arrive, you will be given a placement exam to deter-mine at which level you should be studying. Courses cover all facets of Mexican culture including literature, legends, politics, and dance.

Templo de San Roque

There is also a children's program available. These classes tend to fill up quickly over spring break and in the summertime. Private classes are also available. The school will also set you up with a host family or rent you a nearby casita.

OUTDOOR ADVENTURES

In the mid-18th century Guanajuato suffered from a water shortage, and thus the town council decided to dam an arroyo on the outskirts of the city to help alleviate that problem. They chose a ranch called *La Olla*, or "The Pot," as the site for this dam. The name stuck and the Presa de la Olla opened in 1749, supplying Guanajuato with a constant source of fresh water. Half the cost of the dam was covered by a wealthy mine owner. In 1795, Guanajuato's provincial governor, Juan Antonio de Riaño—who would later take refuge in the Alhóndiga in the battle that made *El Pípila* famous—took note of the beauty around this dam and commissioned a park to be constructed around it. The dam itself continued to provide water to the town and its neighbors until 1895. Today, it is the site of the June festivals of San Juan and the Festival of Presa de la Olla. It is also a beautiful place to spend an afternoon strolling along the Florencio Antillón Park, which features more than 1,000 square feet of gardens crisscrossed by symmetrical paths. At the center of the park, you will find a 17-foot statue of Father Hidalgo, designed in Rome by the artist Guis Trabachi. There is also a local legend that says that, from the Presa de la Olla at twilight, you can make out the profile of a bearded man on the side of the city's Bufa Mountain. According to tradition, this is said to be the profile of Jesus Christ. To get here from the southeast side of town, take Calle Sangre de Cristo from Plaza Allende to Paseo Madero, and then bear left onto Paseo de la Presa. From the northwest side of town, take the Tunel de los Ángeles and take a left when it lets out at Calle Nelayote. At the Monumento a Cervantes roundabout, bear left onto Boulevard Guanajuato and merge onto Carretera Panorámica.

Located on the outskirts of Guanajuato, **Cerro de la Bufa** is considered to be an enchanted place with many legends surrounding it. It is also a popular location for hiking. There are trails that will take you around old quarries that were used to build the city's oldest buildings. There are also a variety of climbing routes suitable for

Cerro de la Bufa.

beginning and advanced climbers. Camping is also allowed here free of charge; however, keep in mind that this is a semidesert climate—the nights can get quite cold. To get to La Bufa, take the Carretera Panorámica toward the regional hospital southwest of Presa de la Olla. Turn east at the electrical substation and the site will be right in front of you. Be sure to bring plenty of water as well as light snacks.

TOURS

Guanajuato Office of Tourism (473-732-1574; www.guanajuato-travel .com) is the main tourist information office in Guanajuato; it is located at the south end of Plaza de la Paz next to the basilica. This office is open daily from 8 AM to 8 PM; it offers information in English about a variety of inexpensive tours around Guanajuato, as well as to the statue of Cristo Rey and other nearby points of interest.

If you plan to take no other tour, you should really set a day aside for a tour of the Paseo de la Independéncia. It costs about $20 for an eight-hour tour that takes you first on a tour of Dolores Hidalgo, makes a brief stop at the sanctuary of Atotonílco, and then on to San Miguel de Allende, where you are set loose for about an hour. The tour does make brief stops at *artesenia* shops and selected ice cream vendors in Dolores (and one gets the sense that the guides get kickbacks for this), but you are not required to purchase anything. The tour's biggest drawback is that the guide picks the place to eat in San Miguel, and it is not always the best restaurant around. In cases such as this, it's best to just wait it out and find a restaurant to your liking once you are set free on the streets of San Miguel.

Keep in mind that while the tourist office in Guanajuato is staffed by people who speak English, most of the tour guides generally do not conduct tours in English. Not to worry—the tours are still well worth the cost in money and time. If you need translation, there is usually at least one fellow sightseer along for the ride who is bilingual. Or, better yet, use this trusty guide to get yourself informed on what's what.

Mellado Horseback Riding (473-105-0417) is a small tour company that offers horseback excursions in the hills surrounding Guanajuato. They will guide you along back trails to spots with breathtaking panoramic views of the city and the surrounding environs. The staff is fully bilingual.

3

Side Trips

DOLORES HIDALGO

THE RELAXED CHARACTER of present-day Dolores Hidalgo is a far cry from the frenzied, chaotic atmosphere that must have prevailed here on the morning of September 16, 1810, when Miguel Hidalgo made what has become known as *el Grito de Dolores* (the Cry of Dolores). It was a call to insurrection against the Spanish powers that ruled Mexico. In the early morning hours, Father Hidalgo ordered the church bells to be rung to gather the people of Dolores. From the balcony of his residence he addressed the crowd, and legend has it that he ended his speech by calling out, *"¡Viva la Virgen de Guadalupe! ¡Viva Fernando VII! ¡Mexicanos, viva México!"* ("Long live Our Lady of Guadalupe! Long live Fernando VII! Mexicans, long live Mexico!") After this speech, he and Don Ignacio Allende gathered their ragtag forces and headed for San Miguel de Allende. It is from this that Dolores Hidalgo has become known throughout Mexico as "the cradle of independence" and Miguel Hidalgo is revered as the father of Mexican independence.

Every year on the night of September 15, thousands of people crowd Mexico City's giant main square, the seat of Mexican government and one-time center of the Aztec empire. At 11 PM, the country's president steps onto the balcony of the national palace overlooking the square and rings the actual bell that Father Hidalgo

LEFT: The central plaza in Dolores Hidalgo is dominated by a statue commemorating Hidalgo himself.

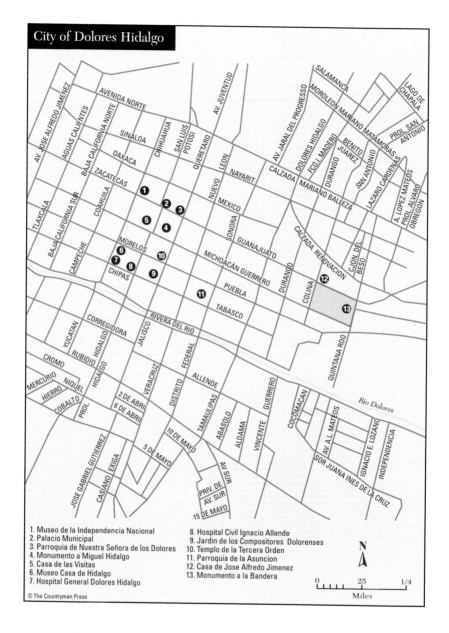

City of Dolores Hidalgo

1. Museo de la Independencia Nacional
2. Palacio Municipal
3. Parroquia de Nuestra Señora de los Dolores
4. Monumento a Miguel Hidalgo
5. Casa de las Visitas
6. Museo Casa de Hidalgo
7. Hospital General Dolores Hidalgo
8. Hospital Civil Ignacio Allende
9. Jardin de los Compositores Dolorenses
10. Templo de la Tercera Orden
11. Parroquia de la Asuncion
12. Casa de Jose Alfredo Jimenez
13. Monumento a la Bandera

N

0   25   1/4
Miles

© The Countryman Press

rang in the predawn hours in 1810. The ceremony reaches its conclusion at midnight with the president repeating Hidalgo's speech, calling out "*Viva*" with the names of people who were vital to the independence, as well as "*¡Viva la independéncia!*" With each call by the president, all of the voices of the crowd call back, "*¡Viva!*" The *Grito* culminates with a high point of "*¡Viva Mexico!*" At that point, the sky lights up with fireworks. Moreover, every six years this ceremony is held in the tiny town where Hidalgo actually made the call for independence, cramming Dolores Hidalgo's main plaza with thousands of people and attracting such dignitaries as the first President Bush in the 1990s.

Obviously, the town of Dolores Hidalgo takes great pride in its role in Mexico's independence. Despite the fact that this is a remote village of barely sixty thousand residents, this town has a *zócalo* (principal plaza) that is one of the most beautiful in Mexico. At its center, you will find a tall bronze statue of Miguel Hidalgo holding aloft the standard of the Virgin Mary in his left hand while extending his right hand as if imploring the onlooker to revolution. This statue is surrounded with a circular walkway lined with benches shaded by various types of trees.

Over Hidalgo's shoulder, the city's main church, Parroquia de Nuestra Señora de los Dolores, looms tall. This magnificent baroque church of pink quarry stone towers over the town of Dolores Hidalgo,

Preparing for a wedding at Parroquia de Nuestra Señora in Dolores Hidalgo.

Ice Cream of Dolores Hidalgo

In the Plaza Principal in the town of Dolores Hidalgo, surrounded by the monuments to Mexico's independence, there is a monument of a different kind. Tucked away in the southwest corner of the plaza, there is a monument to the palate. Here, vendors loiter behind stands filled with some of the best homemade ice cream you will find anywhere. These ice cream stands have become a reason in and of themselves for visiting Dolores Hidalgo. The beautiful plaza is the perfect venue for kicking back and enjoying a large waffle cone of your favorite flavor. Or, better yet, why not take this opportunity to try flavors that you've never had—and likely won't have the chance to try anywhere else.

An ice cream stand in Dolores Hidalgo selling many flavors.

facing out toward the Plaza Principal. It was built in 1778 and has been beautifully preserved through all these years. In its extravagant churrigueresque form are images of Jesus Christ's arrest, trial, and crucifixion. The image of the crucifixion finishes off the set at the cornice, on top of which sits a small clock tower. On each side are columns supporting two bell towers, each containing three rows of arches. These bells ring out each year on Mexico's Independence Day

For just a little over a dollar you can get a small cup of ice cream, or there are larger options available as well. There are, of course, plenty of the more traditional flavors. For the truly timid, there is vanilla, strawberry, or chocolate. There is also mango, pistachio, or caramel with pecans. These are all wonderful flavors and probably a good choice if you're going to have a large cone. However, while you're there you might think about asking for a sample of some of the more unusual flavors that are available. You'll be surprised to find that these strange flavors actually make for some truly interesting ice cream. For example, avocado ice cream is rich and creamy with just the subtle flavor of the green fruit. Corn has bits of corn throughout, but it's not bad. Even mole-flavored ice cream is worth a taste if you otherwise like this traditional dish. Other unusual flavors worth trying include beer and tequila. These two are actually not so much ice cream but rather shaved ice flavored with these beverages. In any case, these flavors are subtle but present—and the taste of alcohol is also present, particularly in the tequila-flavored dessert. Perhaps you don't want to wolf down a large container of this stuff, but it's good for a try. Flavors to stay away from would include pork rind, fish, and shrimp. The shrimp ice cream is particularly disagreeable, with chunks of shrimp throughout. Speaking as someone who loves shrimp, it is not a flavor or texture that lends itself to good ice cream. And when you stop to consider that there aren't any fresh shrimp anywhere near Dolores Hidalgo, you realize that—for the good of your own well-being—this is a delicacy that is better left alone.

That said, if you find yourself in Dolores Hidalgo, take time to sample the local flavors. It's an experience that is unique as well as delicious.

to commemorate the town's most famous event, Hidalgo's call to independence. Inside, there is an altar covered with gold leaf supporting a framed niche containing an image of the Virgin of Guadalupe.

On Sunday afternoons, this plaza fills with a heterogeneous mix of townspeople, old and young, who congregate here to sit in the shade, eat ice cream, and have long conversations. Looking at them, you may be tempted to say to yourself, "When in Rome . . . "

Dolores Hidalgo enjoys a lively central plaza.

Museums

At Calle Morélos #1, the 18th-century home of Miguel Hidalgo is now the **Museo Casa de Don Miguel Hidalgo** (418-182-0723). Several of the rooms have been preserved to authentically re-create the atmosphere at the time of the War of Independence. While many of the items are not originals, many of the items here did belong to Hidalgo—including furniture, garments, and other personal effects. Farther into the house, you will find several shrines and other testaments to Hidalgo and the other heroes of Mexico's independence.

Nearby, an 18th-century building originally used as a prison is now the **Museo de la**

A small statue of Miguel Hidalgo at his former residence in Dolores Hidalgo.

Independéncia Nacional (418-182-0193). On September 16, 1810,

Miguel Hidalgo set the inmates free and bade them to join his cru-
sade for independence. The museum displays several historical and
patriotic objects from that time as well as several paintings, photographs, and other works of fine art. There is also a display dedicated
to José Alfredo Jiménez, the world-famous Mexican folk music com-
poser who was born here.

A patriotic work of art at the Museo de la Independéncia Nacional in Dolores Hidalgo.

Children enjoy the waterslides at Parque Acuatico Splash.

LEÓN

After Mexico's War of Independence, León went through an economic and population boom establishing it as the largest city in the state and one of the country's most important agricultural and industrial zones. Today, León is best known as the shoe capital of Mexico. However, the city is much more than that. It is a city of contrasts, with modern buildings of steel and glass alongside beautifully preserved colonial structures. At its center, you will find beautiful Martyrs' Square surrounded on three sides by neoclassical archways. The León Zoo (477-210-2335; www.zooleon.org.mx) features more than two thousand animals, from polar bears to panthers, and a miniature train. For an interactive science experience, check out the Explora Science Center Museum (477-711-6711; www.explora.mx). This large science park contains four halls, an IMAX theater, and special exhibits.

If you are looking for a fun place to pass some time with the kids on a hot day, check out **Parque Acuatico Splash** (472-748-6030; www.splashleon.com). Located just southeast of León International Airport, this water park offers a wave pool, a children's zone with eight water slides, as well as four slides for the adventurous traveler. There are also several kids' pools and other swimming pools. Once

Cultural Differences

You will find the Mexican people to be, by and large, warm and vivacious. However, it is important to keep in mind that theirs is a different culture from your own, and certain aspects can be quite different. The more familiar you are with these differences, the better you will be at navigating through Mexican culture. For example, Mexicans consider the exchange of proper greetings to be very important. Handshakes are exchanged between men and a cheek-to-cheek embrace is customary between women as well as between men and women, often even if you've just met. Also, it is customary to greet all members of a group individually. A single collective greeting to a group is viewed as both lazy and rude. And even if your Spanish is incredibly poor, Mexicans greatly appreciate any effort you make to speak their language. A quick *Buenas dias* will go a long way to earn you respect in the eyes of local residents. Always remember that family and religion are central to Mexican culture, so avoid making derogatory or critical comments about either. It is also considered to be in poor taste to end a conversation by stating that you soon need to be somewhere else. And keep in mind that siesta falls between 2 PM and 5 PM every day. You'll notice that during this time, many businesses shut down and the town seems to clear out a bit.

In Guanajuato and San Miguel de Allende, many locals are proficient English speakers. However, they will likely be confused by certain aspects of your colloquial English. When conversing in English with locals, try to speak in grammatically correct sentences and avoid using slang. However, don't speak unnecessarily slowly or in disjointed sentences; this can understandably come across as insulting.

Among the things that you may find odd and uncomfortable, Mexicans tend to operate with much less personal space than is customary north of the border. Try to keep this in mind if you find your personal space being encroached upon in casual conversation. Also, Mexicans can be more overtly flirtatious than you may be used to. If you are a woman traveling alone, be prepared for the occasional whistle and teasing comment. Ignore this and avoid getting confrontational; it is not likely to get you anywhere.

you've cooled off, head over to the sea lion show. On top of all the aquatic diversions, this park features a soccer field, basketball court, and other attractions. There is also a hotel on site where you can rent rooms and bungalows for a moderate price. These accommodations are clean and comfortable and feature amenities such as sundecks and Jacuzzis.

CRISTO REY DEL CUBILETE

At the highest point of the mountain known as Cerro del Cubilete, nearly 8,500 feet above sea level and at a point that is purported to be the geographic center of Mexico, you will find one of Mexico's most important religious monuments. Cristo Rey, or Christ the King, is a small chapel topped by a giant, 65-foot bronze art deco statue of Jesus that was built by Nicolás Mariscal in 1944—at the site of a similar but smaller statue that was destroyed during the Cristero War.

The statue holds his arms open as two angels kneel at his feet—presenting him with a crown of thorns and a royal crown, representing martyrdom and glory. These figures rest upon a concrete hemisphere that is meant to represent the universe. A small chapel makes up the base of the statue. Inside, the altar rests upon a circular platform and a large crown hangs above, symbolizing the divine royalty of Christ. The site also provides an extensive view of the entire region. This statue has become one of the most frequented religious sites in Mexico, especially for the feast of Cristo Rey on November 21. The sculpture can be accessed by a paved road that winds up the mountain until it comes to a roundabout underneath the monument.

The statue of Cristo Rey del Cubilete.

Cristo Rey is located about 30 minutes outside of Guanajuato, about halfway to Silao. To get to Cristo Rey, you can sign up for the tour at the tourist office in Guanajuato. The tour lasts about three hours. However, if you'd rather go on your own, there are buses that go up to the shrine from the Guanajuato bus station. These buses make the trip about nine times a day between 6 AM and 6 PM during the week, and even more than that on the weekend. To drive there, take Highway 110 southwest toward Silao for about 10 miles and take the side road to the right, headed to La Valenciana.

SANTUARIO DE ATOTONÍLCO

About 7 miles northeast of San Miguel de Allende is the small but venerated sanctuary of Atotonílco, meaning "place of the hot waters." This site was a hacienda when, in 1740, a priest named Luis Felipe Neri de Alfaro acquired the land and began the construction of the church. Alfaro commissioned an indigenous artist named Miguel Antonio Martínez de Pocasangre to paint murals that have since made this church famous. Over the next 11 years, construction was completed on this impressive chapel. It contained an ornate altar of carved, gold-encrusted wood embellished with paintings on Venetian mirrors. Additionally, the lives of Catholic saints and martyrs and scenes of the Last Judgment are linked by ornate banners and color-ful floral decoration. The church has been referred to as the "Sistine Chapel of the Americas," and almost every square inch of the walls and ceilings inside the sanctuary is covered with fresco paintings in a raucous expression of Mexican folk art. The murals also portray angels, archangels, saints, and demons amid decorations of fanciful flowers and fruits. However, not all of this art is so jovial. There are many images of tortured, suffering souls—as well as a 17th-century statue of Jesus bleeding horribly from his wounds. Years of neglect and environmental degradation have put all the artwork in this sanc-tuary in extremely fragile condition. In fact, the World Monuments Fund has put this church on its list of the world's hundred most endangered monuments.

However, the sanctuary of Atotonílco retains an honored place in Mexican religious culture. It has become a place where worshipers come to make atonement for their sins. Each year, thousands come to participate in such religious practices as sleeping on cold stone floors, crawling around the perimeter of the church on bare and bloodied

Detail from Santuario de Atotonílco.

knees, as well as wearing crowns of thorns and flagellating themselves
with whips. In perhaps the most important annual event held at this
shrine, large crowds of pilgrims walk in a solemn procession from the
Atotonílco shrine to San Miguel de Allende. They carry the statue
known as the Milagrosa Imagen del Señor de la Columna (the Mirac-
ulous Image of The Lord of The Column). It is highly venerated and
has had several miracles attributed to it. In fact, the tradition of the
procession began in the 18th century after San Miguel de Allende
had been hit by an epidemic. A dying merchant asked for the statue
to be brought to him in his final hours. As the story goes, once the
statue was brought into his home, the man recovered and the epidemic broke.

The church is surrounded by a nearly deserted village of extremely poor residents, so a visit to this church is unlikely to be an uplifting
experience. In fact, you are likely to be met by crippled beggars when
you exit the shrine. However, you are unlikely to come away without
being affected in some way. To get here, take Highway 51 north out
of San Miguel de Allende or south out of Dolores Hidalgo. Turn west
off the highway at Rancho Viejo.

A 250-acre ecological reserve is located just outside of San Miguel de Allende. This reserve (415-154-4715; www.elcharco.org.mx) has a wealth of impressive vistas as you explore its abundant plants and wildlife as well as aqueduct ruins that once served the city. Many of the plants you find here are endangered. There are also enormous cliffs that rise up from the foliage that make great places to enjoy majestic landscapes that look over San Miguel, the broad Laja River Valley, and the Sierra de Guanajuato in the distance. The abundance of wildlife here can be found in canyons, where permanent spring waters give rise to a wide range of fauna from cactus to aquatic plants, as well as in wetlands—where the Las Colonias Dam has created a permanent body of water in the heart of the botanical garden. Here, trees and shrubs grow along the water's edge and more than 20 species of migratory birds take shelter. Entrance to the park costs about $0.25 and children under 10 get in free. There is a series of paths that take visitors from the information center located at the entrance to points of interest throughout the reserve. These include the Plaza of the Four Winds, a community and ceremonial space with panoramic views; the impressive cliffs of the canyon; and the reservoir, with its resident and migratory birds. These paths are patrolled by the reserve security staff and are ideal for walking, running, mountain biking, and to access rock climbing areas. Adjacent to the botanical gardens, there is also a nature park that has a recreational area with vehicle access and facilities for camping, picnics, and horseback riding. To get here from downtown San Miguel de Allende, go east on Salida a Querétaro and turn left at the traffic circle with the equestrian statue. Continue straight on the cobbled-stone and dirt roads for about 500 yards, then follow the signs guiding you left to the park. The easiest way to get here using public transportation is to take a taxi.

LA GRUTA

La Gruta is located in a private park 15 minutes out of San Miguel de Allende. This is a series of three caves with a series of pools that are fed by a thermal spring. These pools vary from lukewarm to steaming. These pools are the product of the geothermal activity that is happening under the ground around this region, and they get hotter the farther into the caves you go. Many also believe that these pools have rejuvenating effects on the body. The caves are well-lit and you can swim into them and pick the water temperature that you prefer. There are changing rooms here; you can also rent a locker and eat at a small outdoor restaurant that sells typical Mexican food. You can rent this site between 6 PM and midnight for private parties

The pools at La Gruta.

of up to 10 people. Make reservations through Señora Flor de María Perez (415-185-2099).

SANCTUARIO CAÑADA DE LA VIRGEN

Cañada de la Virgen (415-154-8771; www.canadadelavirgen.com) is an archeological and nature preserve that lies southwest of San Miguel de Allende. The archeological site consists of five groups of pre-Hispanic monuments that were once the northern reaches of the Toltec empire. These monuments include pyramids as high as 60 feet, terraced basements, an ancient ball court, and an avenue that is the length of nearly 11 football fields. These sites have also yielded many smaller artifacts, such as pottery and metal tools, that have been a boon to archeologists trying to piece together the ancient past of this region. However, nine hundred years of neglect have taken their toll on these sites—therefore they are currently not open to the public, though the National Institute of Anthropology and History (INAH) has plans to do so in the near future. However, this area is also one of the largest ex-haciendas in the state of Guanajuato and is ideal for outdoor activities such as hiking, camping, and horseback riding. There is a group in San Miguel de Allende that specializes in eco-tours and spiritual excursions to this location. They offer a wide range of services and tours, though they require guests to sign a wilderness agreement in order to protect the natural habitat. To get here on your own, take the road to Celaya south out of San Miguel de Allende past the Presa de Allende Reservoir. Then take the road to the right and continue for another 9.3 miles.

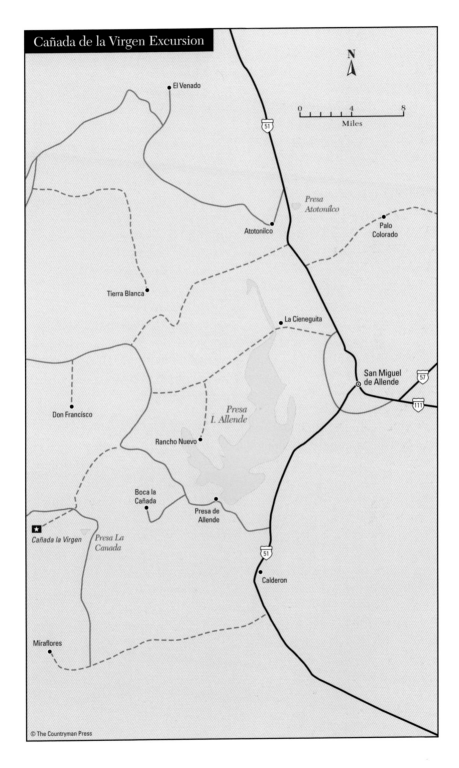

Cañada de la Virgen Excursion

N

0   4   8
Miles

El Venado

51

Presa
Atotonílco

Palo
Colorado

Atotonílco

Tierra Blanca

La Cieneguita

San Miguel
de Allende

57

111

Don Francísco

Presa
I. Allende

Rancho Nuevo

Boca la
Cañada

Presa de
Allende

★ Cañada la Virgen

Presa La
Canada

51

Calderon

Miraflores

© The Countryman Press

SIERRA DE LOBOS

Located about 34 miles northwest of Guanajuato and only 18 miles north of the city of León is the Sierra de Lobos Nature Reserve (477-774-2121). This reserve is an area of more than 250,000 acres and has been important for the protection and preservation of the Mexican wolf, which is also how this area got its name. Other animals that call this reserve home include pumas, white-tailed deer, flying squirrels, and a wide variety of birds. There are also numerous trails in the park that will lead you along sheer cliffs and dams located within the park. If you are interested in an extended stay, there are also hotels located within the reserve. The grounds of this nature reserve are full of crags, ponds, and mountain streams, making it ideal for a wide range of outdoor activities—including rock climbing, fishing, hiking, and camping. However, keep in mind that it rains here fairly regularly during the summer and gets quite cold during the winter. To get here, take Highway 37-S north from León toward Ocampo and look for the signs. You can get here via public transportation by going to the central bus station in León and taking the bus to Ocampo. Tell the bus driver you want to get off at Vergel de la Sierra. Here you will find a hotel and visitors center that offers guided tours for a nominal fee. Or, if you prefer, hike the trails independently.

Hiking at Sierra de Lobos.

About 54 miles south of Guanajuato off of Highway 110 and Highway 45, you will find the protected ecological zone of Valle de Santiago. There is a village here called Camébaro, which was settled in 1607. Later in the 17th century, the Hospital de Tarascos was established here to care for the indigenous people who had fallen victim to a devastating epidemic of disease. The region is pocked with volcanic craters and blessed with various microclimates, which have given rise to a wide array of wildlife. In fact, it is sometimes referred to as the *Siete Luminares,* or the Seven Lights, because of the seven volcanic craters in the area. These include La Alberca, which is famous for its sulfur waters; La Hoya de Cintura, filled with thermal springs; and La Hoya de las Flores, where you will find vestiges of a pre-Hispanic ceremonial town as well as several springs. And then there is a crater named Parangueo el Viejo, which has a tunnel that is nearly 1,000 feet long that leads to a salt lake in the interior. The terrain here is mountainous, with volcanic rock formations ranging from 6 feet to 66 feet high, making it ideal for hiking, rappelling, mountain biking, and other outdoor activities.

ZONA RECREATIVA DE LAS PALOMAS

Fifteen minutes north of Guanajuato off Highway 110, you will come upon the nature reserve of Las Palomas in La Cuenca de la Esperanza (473-732-0294). This is a vast wildlife preserve and recreational zone popular with nature enthusiasts. It lies on the migratory path of several species of neotropical birds from as far away as Alaska. There are said to be 172 different species of birds in this preserve, almost half of which are migratory. There are also other interesting animal species, such as white-tailed deer and lynx. This reserve is crisscrossed by a series of rugged trails that are ideal for birdwatchers and naturalists as well. These trails will also lead you to some of Guanajuato's most famous mines, such as the La Valenciana, the Mina de Guadalupe, and the Real de Santa Ana. The preserve has trained guides that can provide you with in-depth information about the birds as well as the rest of the flora and fauna of the Guanajuato Sierras for a nominal fee. In recent years, this area has seen development to accommodate increasing interest. There are now facilities here where you can rent bicycles, binoculars, camping gear, and even cottages; there are also sanitary facilities, food vendors, and marked camping areas.

4

Information

EMBASSIES

U.S. Embassy
(01-55) 5080-2000
Reforma #305, Mexico City D.F.
06500
Open: Mon.–Fri. 9 AM–2 PM
and 3 PM–5 PM

Canadian Embassy
(01-55) 5724-7900 or 800-706-2900
Schiller #529, Mexico City D.F.
11560
Open: Mon.–Fri. 9 AM–1 PM
and 2 PM–5 PM

EMERGENCY SERVICES

Guanajuato
Emergency
Dial 068

Police Department
473-732-0292
Alhóndiga #10, Guanajuato, Gto.
36000

Fire Department
473-732-3357
Pozuelos s/n, Guanajuato, Gto.
36000

Ángeles Verdes (Ambulance)
473-732-0119
Casa Martha s/n, Guanajuato,
Gto. 36000

State Office of Tourism
473-732-1574
Plaza de la Paz #14, Guanajuato,
Gto. 36000

LEFT: There are no dull views in Guanajuato. Maria Miller K sska

U.S. Consulate
415-152-2357
Hernández Macías #72, San
Miguel de Allende, Gto. 37700
Open: Mon.–Fri. 9 AM–1 PM;
closed Mexican and American
holidays

Emergency Hotline
in English
415-152-2890
Available: Mon.–Fri. 8 AM–4 PM

Police Department
415-120-4524
Salida a Querétaro, San Miguel
de Allede, Gto. 37700

Fire Department
415-152-3238
Salida a Querétaro, San Miguel
de Allede, Gto. 37700

Red Cross (Ambulance)
415-152-1616
Libaramiento Zavala Zavala s/n,
San Miguel de Allede, Gto.
37700

BANKS

Guanajuato

Banamex
473-732-1707
Calle los Ángeles #21, Guanajua-
to, Gto. 36000
Open: Mon.–Fri. 9 AM–4 PM;
Sat. 10 AM–2 PM
Features two 24-hour ATMs.

Banorte
473-732-9222
Calle Alhóndiga #10, Guanajua-
to, Gto. 36000
Open: Mon.–Fri. 9 AM–4 PM;
Sat. 10 AM–2 PM
Money exchange hours are
Monday through Friday
9 AM–1:30 PM. Features one
24-hour ATM.

HBC
473-732-0187
Plaza de la Paz #59, Guanajuato,
Gto. 36000
Open: Mon.–Sat. 8 AM–7 PM
Features two 24-hour ATMs.

Serfin-Santander
473-732-7385
Avenida Juárez #13, Guanajuato,
Gto. 36000
Open: Mon.–Fri. 9 AM–3 PM
Features one 24-hour ATM.

San Miguel de Allende

Banamex
415-152-1040
Canal #4, San Miguel de
Allende, Gto. 37700
Open: Mon.–Fri. 9 AM–4 PM;
Sat. 10 AM–2 PM
Features three 24-hour ATMs.

Banorte
415-152-0019
San Francisco #17, San Miguel
de Allende, Gto. 37700
Open: Mon.–Fri. 9 AM–4 PM;
Sat. 9:30 AM–2:30 PM

Money exchange hours are Monday through Friday 9 AM–1:30 PM. Features one 24-hour ATM.

Bancomer
415-152-0847
Juárez #11, San Miguel de Allende, Gto. 37700
Open: Mon.–Fri. 8:30 AM–4 PM Features two 24-hour ATMs. A photocopy machine is also available during bank hours.

HBC
415-152-0847
San Francisco #31, San Miguel de Allende, Gto. 37700
Open: Mon.–Sat. 8 AM–7 PM Features one 24-hour ATM.

Serfin-Santander
415-152-1161
San Francisco #32, San Miguel de Allende, Gto. 37700
Open: Mon.–Fri. 9 AM–3 PM Features one 24-hour ATM.

BUS TERMINALS

Guanajuato
Central de Autobuses
473-733-1329
Carretera a Silao #8, Guanajuato, Gto. 36000

San Miguel de Allende
Central de Autobuses
415-152-2206
Calzada de la Estación #90, San Miguel de Allende, Gto. 37700

CALLING HOME AND MEXICO

To call directly to the United States from Mexico, dial 001 then the area code and phone number. Conversely, to call Mexico from the United States, dial 011-52 then the area code and phone number.

It isn't a good idea to dial direct long-distance or international calls from your hotel room in Mexico. Hotels often add their own surcharges, even to local calls. This also applies to bringing and using your cell phone while in Mexico. It may seem extremely convenient to pull your phone out of your pocket and dial away, but you will likely wish you hadn't at the end of the month when you get a phone bill packed with hefty international roaming charges. Even receiving calls on your cell can result in excessive charges. Public phones in the larger towns are provided by a company called Ladatel; it offers long-distance calls with a *tarjeta de teléfono* (phone card) issued through TelMex, the national phone company of Mexico. You can buy prepaid Ladatel phone cards in pharmacies, convenience stores, and supermarkets. Another option is to obtain a calling card through your own phone company before leaving on your trip.

ELECTRICITY

Mexico's electrical system is the same as in the United States and Canada: 110 volts AC. The outlets are compatible with any electrical appliance, recharger, or extension cords you may bring. However, older or smaller hotels may not have outlets suitable for polarized plugs (in which one prong is slightly larger than the other). Pick up an adapter at any hardware or discount store before your trip.

GETTING MARRIED IN MEXICO

As "destination weddings" have become more of a popular practice in the United States, San Miguel de Allende has become an increasingly popular destination to hold such an event. Not only is the city the perfect setting for a storybook wedding, but other Mexican hotspots are nearby, making for a great honeymoon. And if you're going to ask your guests to do some traveling anyway, why not bring them to a place as interesting and wonderful as San Miguel de Allende?

As with any wedding (outside of Las Vegas), getting married in Mexico requires planning, coordination, and the completion of documents. One solution to make the process easier is to complete the legal paperwork in the United States and simply perform the ceremony in Mexico. However, if you want your ceremony to be more than symbolic, there are several requirements that you need to fulfill at the location in Mexico where you will be married.

Keep in mind that religious weddings are not officially recognized in Mexico and thus do not change your legal marriage status. Therefore, in order to have your wedding legally recognized in Mexico and back home, you'll need a civil ceremony performed by a Spanish-speaking judge who resides in the city where you are getting married. You can also arrange to have this ceremony performed at an outside site for an additional fee.

In addition to the judge, you'll need at least two witnesses who are 18 or older, and you'll need to fulfill several other legal requirements for your marriage to be legally binding. To complete these requirements, it is necessary to arrive in Mexico several days before the ceremony. You'll need certified copies of your birth certificates as well as passports and copies of your tourist cards. If you have been married previously, you'll need papers indicating that you have been legally divorced for at least a year. There is also medical lab work that needs to be performed in Mexico.

With all of these ancillary details, it's probably a really good idea to hire a wedding coordinator to help out, especially if you don't speak Spanish. Several wedding planners work out of San Miguel de Allende, and many of the hotels in the city offer their own wedding planners. Check the hotel Web sites for more details.

The following are some wedding planners that you might want to check out:

Celebrations San Miguel
415-154-8367
(U.S.) 512-351-4537
www.celebrationssanmiguel.com
Centro, San Miguel de Allende, Gto. 37700
This company is owned and run by an experienced wedding planner from Austin, Texas. They offer complete wedding planning services and several wedding packages. They will also work with you to scout out the best location in San Miguel to meet your needs.

San Miguel Weddings
415-154-8121
www.sanmiguelweddings.com
Coda #5-A, San Miguel de Allende, Gto. 37700
This company offers a bilingual staff as well as creative catering and equipment rental. They will help you with your itinerary, set appointments, and plan the ceremony and reception.

Los Secretos
415-152-0823
(U.S.) 706-659-2054
www.smasecretos.com
Centro, San Miguel de Allende, Gto. 37700
This business offers a full host of wedding planning services, including photography, music, and hotel reservations.

Weddings San Miguel
415-152-5807
www.weddingssanmiguel.com
Jesús #23, San Miguel de Allende, Gto. 37700
Owned and run by Kris Rudolph, the owner of the Buen Café, who has been catering weddings in San Miguel de Allende for over 10

years. She offers a full range of wedding planning services. Her knowledge of local venues, regulations, and traditions are invaluable for making your wedding go off without a hitch.

INTERNET ACCESS

If you plan on bringing a laptop computer, many hotels offer wireless Internet access as part of their amenities. However, there is always an added risk when traveling with a laptop. For an alternate option, there are several cyber cafés in both San Miguel de Allende and Guanajuato that offer Internet access for a nominal fee (recommendations are listed below). In Guanajuato, these tend to be concentrated near the university, along Calle Positos, and near the

Bagel Cafetín is a great place to get online and grab breakfast.

Plaza San Roque. If you do use these machines, it's always a good idea to click on "Internet Options" and clear the cache before logging off. You don't want any of your personal information sitting on the computer after you have left. However, your best bet is to log into personal accounts sparingly on public computers, since unscrupulous hackers have been known to bug computers in cyber cafés and even hotels with software designed to gain access to personal information—especially banking and e-trade accounts.

Guanajuato

Grumara
473-732-0607
Jardín Reforma #12, Guanajuato, Gto. 36000
Open: Mon.–Sat. 10 AM–10 PM
This Internet café has about a half dozen computer stations and a printer available.

Internet Station Y2K

473-732-1478

Juan Valle #4, Guanajuato, Gto. 36000

Open: Mon.–Sat. 9 AM–11:30 PM

This public Internet café is often filled with college kids—but if you can get to a station, they do have high-speed Internet connections here.

Juan Arturo Reyes Posada

473-733-9588

Calle 28 de Septiembre s/n, Guanajuato, Gto. 36000

Open: Mon.–Sat. 9 AM–11:30 PM

This is kind of a hole-in-the-wall, but they have several computer stations equipped with high-speed Internet access as well as a printer.

San Miguel de Allende

Café Etc.

415-154-8636

Reloj #37, San Miguel de Allende, Gto. 37700

Open: Mon.–Sat. 9 AM–7 PM

This café has about a half dozen computers with DSL connections; a scanner and printer are also available. They sell sandwiches and espresso drinks as well, and have a bilingual staff.

Estación Internet

415-152-7312

Correo #12-A, San Miguel de Allende, Gto. 37700

Open: Daily 9 AM–9 PM

This computer center has several computers available for rental at an hourly rate. There is also a printer and scanner available.

Internet San Miguel

415-100-3077

Mesones #57, San Miguel de Allende, Gto. 37700

Open: Mon.–Sat. 9 AM–9 PM; Sun. 10 AM–6 PM

This cyber café—located in the city's historic center—has eight PCs with high-speed Internet connections, as well as a public Ethernet port for customers with laptops. You can also get espresso drinks, desserts, fresh juices, and even beer and wine. The staff is bilingual, so that's also a plus.

Punto G
415-152-4493
Hidalgo #23, San Miguel de
Allende, Gto. 37700
Open: Daily 9 AM–midnight
This computer center features
14 computer stations with high-
speed Internet connections.
They also have inexpensive
international phone service as
well as bilingual staff.

Quick tip: When approaching someone for information, don't forget to greet them with the time-appropriate salutation (*buenos días, buenas tardes, buenas noches*), even if it's the only Spanish you can think of at the moment. Try not to say simply *"Hola,"* which comes across as abrupt.

LANGUAGE

It goes without saying that Spanish is the primary language spoken in this region of Mexico (though you do find indigenous people who primarily speak native languages). You will likely find that English is only spoken by the better-educated upper class, those who have spent time working in the United States, and those locals who deal with tourists on a daily basis. All in all, this is probably less than 10 percent

The central square in San Miguel de Allende bustles with activity.

of the urban population, even in San Miguel de Allende. This doesn't mean that they won't try to communicate with you in English—the ability to speak English is a valued skill in Mexico and people want to practice at every chance they get. But you will often find that they run through the English phrases they know pretty quickly. Your waiter will understand the names of the items you order off the menu, but he probably won't be able to describe them to you or tell you exactly how they are prepared. This doesn't mean that you won't be able to get along here without knowing any Spanish. In fact, there are many expatriates who live in San Miguel de Allende full-time who don't speak Spanish. However, knowing some Spanish will likely enrich your experience and can really come in handy if you find yourself in a pinch. It is worth your while to make an attempt to learn at least the most basic Spanish phrases. Not only will this help you communicate better, it will also go a long way toward ingratiating you with your Mexican hosts. And that's never a bad thing.

HELPFUL PHRASES

Good morning.	*Buenos días.*
Good afternoon.	*Buenas tardes.*
Good evening. (after 8 PM)	*Buenas noches.*
Goodbye.	*Adios.*
Please.	*Por favor.*
Thank you very much.	*Muchas gracias.*
You're welcome.	*De nada.*
Do you speak English?	*¿Habla usted ingles?*
I don't understand.	*No entiendo.*
How do you say . . . in Spanish?	*¿Como se llama . . . en español?*
My name is . . .	*Me llamo . . .*
Where is . . . ?	*¿Dónde está . . . ?*
To the right.	*A la derecha.*
To the left.	*A la izquierda.*
Straight ahead.	*Derecho.*
What is the rate?	*¿A cuanto es?*
Shower	*Ducha*
Towels	*Toallas*
Soap	*Jabón*
Toilet paper	*Papel higiénico*
Key	*Llave*

Order	*Orden*
Fork	*Tenedor*
Spoon	*Cuchara*
Knife	*Cuchillo*
Napkin	*Servilleta*
Food	*Comida*
Coffee	*Café*
Tea	*Té*
Beer	*Cerveza*
Wine	*Vino*
Milk	*Leche*
Juice	*Jugo*
Money	*Dinero*
Expensive	*Caro*
Cheap	*Barato*
Post office	*Correo*
Driver's licence	*Licencia de manejar*
Gas station	*Gasolinera*
Border	*Frontera*
Passport	*Pasaporte*

LAUNDRY SERVICE

Guanajuato

Lavanderia Alfa
473-733-0766
Amezquita #8, Guanajuato, Gto.
36000
Open: Mon.–Fri. 9 AM–7 PM
Offers dry cleaning, ironing,
and regular washing service.

**Lavanderia Automatica
Internacional**
473-732-6718
Manuel Doblado #28, Guanajua-
to, Gto. 36000
Open: Mon.–Fri. 8 AM–8 PM
Offers same-day service.

San Miguel de Allende

Express Laundry
415-152-7086
Canal #127, San Miguel de
Allende, Gto. 37700
Open: Mon.–Fri. 8 AM–8 PM;
Sat. 9 AM–2 PM
Offers same-day service with
free pickup and delivery.

La Pila
415-152-5810
Jesús #25, San Miguel de
Allende, Gto. 37700
Open: Mon.–Fri. 9 AM–7 PM;
Sat. 9 AM–2 PM
Offers dry cleaning service as

well as regular laundry service. They will pick up and deliver.

Lavandería El Reloj
415-152-3843
Reloj #34-A, San Miguel de Allende, Gto. 37700
Open: Mon.–Fri. 8 AM–8 PM; Sat. 9 AM–2 PM
Reasonable prices and friendly service.

Lavandería Franco
415-154-4495
Zacateros #54-B, San Miguel de Allende, Gto. 37700
Open: Mon.–Fri. 9 AM–7 PM; Sat. 9 AM–5 PM
Offers same-day service with free pickup and delivery.

MAIL

Guanajuato
Post Office
473-732-7394
Calle Ayuntamiento #25, Guanajuato, Gto. 36000
Open: Mon.–Fri. 8 AM–6 PM; Sat. 8 AM–1 PM

Copia Todo
473-732-2356
Avenida Juárez #8, Guanajuato, Gto. 36000
Open: Mon.–Fri. 9 AM–6:30 PM; Sat. 10 AM–3 PM
This shop offers a full range of copy and fax services.

San Miguel de Allende
Post Office
415-152-0089
Calle Correo #16 (one block east of Jardín Principal), San Miguel de Allende, Gto. 37700
Open: Mon.–Fri. 8 AM–4 PM; Sat. 8 AM–noon

Border Crossings
415-152-2497
Mesones #57, San Miguel de Allende, Gto. 37700
Open: Mon.–Fri. 9 AM–6:30 PM; Sat. 10 AM–3 PM
This mailing store is located 1 block off the Jardín Principal. It offers packing and UPS shipping service and has a copy machine, wireless Internet access, and offers mailboxes for rental.

Solutions
415-152-6152
Recreo #11, San Miguel de Allende, Gto. 37700
Open: Mon.–Fri. 9 AM–6 PM; Sat. 9 AM–2 PM
This store offers shipping services including DHL, FedEx, and UPS. They also offer packing and storage services.

MEDICAL SERVICES

Guanajuato
Centro Medico la Presa
473-731-1135
Paseo de la Presa #85, Guanajuato, Gto. 36000

This private medical center offers a full range of health care services.

Hospital General de Guanajuato
473-733-1573
Carretera de Cuota Guanajuato-Silao Km 6.5, Guanajuato, Gto. 36000
This is the public hospital of Guanajuato.

Medica Integral Guanajuatense
473-732-2305
Plaza de la Paz #20, Guanajuato, Gto. 36000
This centrally located medical clinic has specialists in the fields of internal medicine and plastic surgery.

San Miguel de Allende

Hospital Civil
415-152-0045
Reloj #56, San Miguel de Allende, Gto. 37700
This is the public hospital in San Miguel.

Hospital de la Fé
415-152-2329
Libramiento a Dolores Hidalgo #43, San Miguel de Allende, Gto. 37700
This is a private medical center serving the San Miguel area.

MONEY AND MONEY EXCHANGE

American dollars are accepted in some places in Guanajuato and San Miguel de Allende. However, your money will go further if you use pesos. For both convenience and the fact that you don't have much choice, prices are usually rounded off to equal 10 pesos to the dollar. This means that since the official exchange rate is currently fluctuating at more than 10.9 pesos for every dollar, you will generally be overpaying about 9 cents for every dollar you spend.

Mexican currency notes come in denominations of 20, 50, 100, 200, 500, and 1,000. Breaking larger bills is a persistent problem in Mexico, particularly at smaller independent establishments. I once had to wait a half hour after finishing a meal while the restaurant owner ran around to nearby businesses trying to make change for a 500 peso note. The best strategy to avoid such a situation is to pay with larger bills when spending money at larger businesses and save your smaller bills and *monedas* (coins) for small establishments and street vendors.

The quickest and easiest way to get Mexican currency is simply to go to a Mexican ATM and withdraw pesos. Like many banks north of the border, ATMs are located in an entrance area between the outer and inner doors to the bank. After normal business hours—as is the case in the United States—insert your card into the slot next to the outer door, and you will be buzzed inside to do your withdrawal. Once you withdraw currency in Mexican denominations, your bank will convert it back to the dollar amount and charge you that way. These machines generally offer cash at the wholesale bank rate instead of the less-favorable tourist rate that you get when you trade cash or travelers checks, making ATMs both convenient and (on the surface) financially favorable. However, keep in mind that when you use your debit card your bank may charge you a foreign transaction fee of up to 3 percent of the transaction. On top of that, the owner of the ATM will likely charge you a fee of up to 3 percent as well.

Before your trip, it's a good idea to shop around for a credit card that imposes a small foreign transaction fee or none at all. Foreign transaction fees are disclosed in the terms and conditions. In any case, it's probably not such a good idea to rely solely on ATMs as your source for money. You should always have a little extra cash on you in case of an emergency. Banks or *casas de cambio* (exchange houses) offer respectable exchange rates; hotels offer the worst exchange rates. It's always a good idea to exchange at least $50 or $75 into pesos before leaving the United States so that you'll arrive in Mexico with pesos for your cab ride or a meal. Credit cards are widely accepted in San Miguel de Allende and Guanajuato. However, in smaller towns an acceptance of credit cards is less common. The benefit of using a credit card is that you will receive the more favorable wholesale rate. The drawback is that if you're spending money in a place that accepts credit cards, chances are that it's an establishment that is geared toward serving tourists—and thus you get less bang for your buck than at places that cater to locals.

Guanajuato

Divisas Dimas
473-732-1058
Avenida Juárez #33-A, Guanajuato, Gto. 36000
Open: Mon.–Fri. 9 AM–6 PM;
Sat. 9 AM–2 PM

Servicios Populares
de Irapuat
473-732-6137
Madero #6, Guanajuato, Gto. 36000
Open: Mon.–Fri. 9 AM–4 PM;
Sat., Sun. 10 AM–2 PM

San Miguel de Allende

Dicambios Foreign Currency Exchange
415-152-3657
Correo #13, San Miguel de Allende, Gto. 37700
Open: Mon.–Fri. 9 AM–4 PM; Sat., Sun. 10 AM–2 PM

INTERCAM Casa de Cambio
415-154-6676

San Francisco #4, San Miguel de Allende, Gto. 37700
Open: Mon.–Fri. 9 AM–6 PM; Sat. 9 AM–2 PM

Monex
415-154-9996
www.monex.com.mx
Mesones #80, San Miguel de Allende, Gto. 37700
Open: Mon.–Fri. 9 AM–3 PM

Tipping

Being a former waiter, I am all too familiar with the frustration of foreign tourists skipping out without tipping just because they aren't familiar with the local customs. That's just a bad excuse to be cheap. Furthermore, Mexico does not have the same labor laws that you find in the United States and there may be times when your waiter is earning tips and tips alone. Be polite, and plan on tipping service personnel the customary amount.

Bellboys should be tipped based on the pieces of luggage they carry to your room. Restaurant servers are customarily tipped around 15 percent of the total bill; however, if you're dining with a large group, a service charge may be automatically added to the bill. The tipping of chambermaids is optional though highly appreciated. You should tip the gas station attendant about $0.50 and/or let them keep the change when it equals less than a peso. If you take a tour, it's

Tip restaurant servers around 15 percent.

standard to tip the guide about 10 percent of the cost of the trip. This is particularly important if you have a guide who goes out of their way to make sure that you are well informed and have a good time. Taxi drivers are generally not tipped in Mexico, except if they give special service or provide you with good advice. Even then, it is at your discretion, since many taxi drivers will bend over backward to give you advice even if you're not looking for it.

NEWSPAPERS

Atención San Miguel
www.atencionsanmiguel.org
Insurgentes #25, San Miguel de Allende, Gto. 37700
This bilingual newspaper comes out every Friday. It is published by the American staff at the Biblioteca Publica. It costs about $0.75.

PHARMACIES

Guanajuato
Farmacia Isseg
473-732-8248
Avenida Juárez #129-A, Guanajuato, Gto. 36000
Open 24 hours

Farmacia Regina
473-732-1001
Plaza de la Paz #38, Guanajuato, Gto. 36000
Open: Daily 9 AM–2:30 PM and 4 PM–8:30 PM

Farmacia San Francisco
473-732-3915
Alhóndiga #10, Guanajuato, Gto. 36000
Open: Daily 10:30 AM–11 PM

San Miguel de Allende
Botica Agundis

415-152-1198
Canal #26, San Miguel de Allende, Gto. 37700
Open: Daily 10:30 AM–11 PM

Botica de Santa Teresita
415-152-0147
Reloj #28, San Miguel de Allende, Gto. 37700
Open: Daily 9 AM–2:30 PM and 4 PM–8:30 PM

Farmacia Guadalajara
415-154-9047
Ancha de San Antonio #13, San Miguel de Allende, Gto. 37700
Open 24 hours

Farmacia Guanajuato
415-154-6090
Insurgentes #74, San Miguel de Allende, Gto. 37700
Open 24 hours

Poverty in Guanajuato

You will read over and over again throughout this book that the cities of Dolores Hidalgo, Guanajuato, and San Miguel de Allende are beautiful. This is without a doubt true. However, it is important to remember that these are not prefabricated amusement parks. They are real cities with real histories and real people living in them with real problems. And one aspect of those histories and the current living conditions is that Guanajuato is one of the poorest states in Mexico, a country where nearly half the population lives on less than $1,800 a year. This is an important reason why so many Americans can claim an ancestral heritage here. Guanajuato has contributed more than its share of people to the vegetable fields and restaurant kitchens of the United States.

Poverty is a fact of life for many in Mexico.

When visiting, you will see beggars on the sidewalks—including very old women in indigenous dress, women with several children, blind men, men in wheelchairs, women missing limbs, and children

SEASONAL EVENTS

The high season for traveling in Guanajuato and San Miguel de Allende is really determined by their festivals. The first tourist bump of the year comes a couple weeks before Easter and lasts until the week after Easter. During this time, festivals and cultural events fall one on top of the other—with crowds first jamming the streets of Guanajuato that Thursday for *Día de las Flores* (Flower Day) and the Friday of Sorrows the next day. The next week during *Semana Santa* (Holy Week) vacation season gets under way throughout Mexico—

selling chewing gum. There is always the possibility that you will be approached for money. Of course, how you handle this situation is completely up to you. However, it may be a good idea to consider this before the situation arises. Certainly, this problem is not nearly as bad as it was just 10 or 15 years ago. In the mid-1990s, Mexico's economy was in an unusually poor state and destitute indigenous people came to the cities to panhandle and sell trinkets and gum to tourists. One day, I sat in a café in the Jardín de la Unión talking with some Americans that I had just met. Every now and then children would approach us asking for change, and one member of the group would tell these kids quite forcefully (in English) to get lost. While no one would have faulted him for saying no, it was clear that people around us found his behavior to be quite offensive, and I'm sure that it reflected poorly on everyone sitting at the table. Several days later I was in Dolores Hidalgo with a tour group. There was also a couple from Texas along, whose families had come from the area many years before and had done quite well in the United States. When they were approached by a girl asking for money, the woman proudly took her wallet out of her purse and handed the girl a $10 bill. This was shortly followed by the approach of a young boy, to whom she quickly gave $1. Within minutes, the woman was being hounded by women and children asking for money.

These are situations that you will almost certainly not encounter today. While there are a few panhandlers in the cities, it is nowhere near the level of a decade ago. However, they are there. And if you are approached, however you decide to deal with them, it's probably best to do it discreetly.

and San Miguel de Allende is among the country's most popular destinations for Easter festivities. In the fall, this region sees another spike in tourism with Independence Day celebrations in mid-September—and of course the Cerventino Festival, which lasts nearly the entire month of October. For Guanajuato, this is by far the busiest time of the year. Finally, the region is heavily visited again at the end of the year with Christmas celebrations. San Miguel de Allende in particular is known for its beautiful and joyful Christmas festivities.

León (February)

This road race was started in 1979 by the two largest auto clubs in Mexico. It was originally held in the state of Mexico, but in 1998 it was moved to León, Guanajuato. Today this is an annual event in León, where it has an extremely compact route and attracts crews from around the world. The dirt roads in the mountainous region north of the city are perfect for sending cars flying over bumps and sliding around corners. The city's modern Poliforum Expo Center at Boulevard Adolfo López Mateos and Boulevard Francisco Villa hosts the rally headquarters and service park, where fans can examine the cars close up and meet the drivers and crews. There are also fiesta ceremonies held in the city of Guanajuato. For more information, call 477-771-2530 or visit the Web site at www.rallymexico.com.

Fiesta del Señor de la Conquista (Lord of the Conquest Feast)

San Miguel de Allende (First Friday in March)

This solemn celebration is in honor of the Holy Christ of the Conquest, a figure which was presented to the town of San Miguel by the King of Spain and brought by Franciscan monks in the 16th century from the town of Pátzcuaro, Michoacán, where it was carved. Today, this work of art can be found in one of the altars of the Parroquia de San Miguel. The Thursday before the feast, a parade of bulls decorated with flowers, fruits, and other items symbolizing fertility marches through town. This parade is accompanied by music, fireworks, and dancing. The next day, residents customarily attend mass—followed by traditional dances in the Jardín Principal. Later in the afternoon, people make offerings of bread and sugar, known as *parandes*, to the image of the Señor de la Conquista. In some parts of the city, the feast goes on through Saturday and Sunday.

Viernes de Dolores (Friday of Sorrows)

Guanajuato (Weekend before Holy Week)

In the days leading up to this celebration, residents set up altars for the Virgen Dolorosa (Sorrowful Virgin). These altars can be seen in churches, private homes, businesses, and even government buildings. The celebration itself is actually anything but sorrowful, except possibly for the person who has to clean up afterward. Thursday afternoon is devoted to cleaning and repairing public spaces in preparation for the coming festivities. On Thursday night, people crowd the streets

A band plays in Plazuela San Fernando.

and partake of fresh fruits and juices. In Guanajuato, people arrive from the countryside and set up shop in the Plaza de la Paz with stands selling flowers, handicrafts, and food. They work in shifts around the clock over the next couple days, sleeping when they can right there on the street. Crowds of people jam the streets during this time doing the traditional *baile de las flores,* in which young men are expected to give flowers to their female friends. On Friday, many people attend solemn religious ceremonies, but festivities continue through the weekend.

Semana Santa (Holy Week)

San Miguel de Allende (Week of Easter)

Throughout Mexico, the week of Easter and the week after (*Semana Pascua*) is the time of the year to take vacations, and Guanajuato is a very popular region in which to spend that vacation. For this reason, hotel rates throughout the area are significantly higher during this time. San Miguel de Allende is considered one of the best places in Mexico to come to experience two solid weeks of processions, parties, prayers, pageantry, and pyrotechnics. The most remarkable of these events takes place on Good Friday, with a huge procession organized by the town's churches. Roman centurions parade through town astride their horses, ahead of floats and effigies of biblical figures. Amazingly, this is followed by a man portraying Jesus who drags a heavy cross as blood drips from his forehead, which bears a real crown of thorns.

Fiestas of San Juan and Presa de la Olla

Guanajuato (End of June, Beginning of July)

On the days leading up to Saint's Feast Day, a large arts festival is held at the Presa de la Olla outside of town. There are all sorts of festivities, including music, dancing, and lots of food. On the actual day of the feast (June 24), people show up to picnic and enjoy a fireworks show. A couple weeks later, on the first Monday of July, the crowds return to Presa de la Olla to celebrate the annual opening of the floodgates. This celebration has been held since the dam was built, when the reservoir periodically had to be drained. Guanajuato's mayor and the governor participate, signaling the opening of the floodgates—when a rushing waterfall pours out of the dam. There are

Enjoying a ride during a festival in Guanajuato.

many festivities that go along with this event—including a traditional waltz performed by the state band at the moment the floodgates are opened.

International Guitar Festival

San Miguel de Allende (July)
This festival is a celebration of the guitar and the role this diverse instrument has played in different cultures. People come to San Miguel from all over the world to play all styles of guitar music, including classical, Spanish, jazz, and modern. In addition to these performances, musicians also host workshops, classes, and lectures on the art of guitar playing.

San Antonio de Padua

San Miguel de Allende (Sunday after July 13)
This celebration is also known as the *fiesta de los locos y hortelanos,* or the party of the insane and the farmers. It takes place in the crowded neighborhood of San Antonio. Tradition has it that this day of dancing is an offering to saints who have healed you or helped you out during the year. However, today the dancing is done purely for the pleasure of it—resulting in a crowd of insane people. People traverse the neighborhood in decorated carts, dressed in colorful or bizarre costumes.

Día de la Cueva (Cave Day)

Guanajuato (July 31)
This celebration is held in honor of Saint Ignatius of Loyola, founder of the Jesuit order; the Jesuits played a crucial role in the founding of the city of Guanajuato. The celebration takes place in a cave in the nearby hills of Cerro de los Picachos. Processions to the cave begin the night of July 30, when the hills become illuminated by flashlights and candles. Participants who do not go that evening do so the next day.

On Día de la Cueva, hundreds of people climb to the top of Cerro de la Bufa.

There are vendors and food sellers set up all along the way. Celebrations include a country fair, traditional dances, and fireworks.

Festival de la Independencia

Dolores Hidalgo (September)

In the month of September, the town of Dolores Hidalgo stops to celebrate the vital role their town played in the independence of Mexico. This celebration is marked by a variety of cultural and artistic events. The most important of these takes place on the evening of September 15, when crowds gather in the town square for the traditional *grita de independencia* (cry for independence). Every six years Mexico's president comes to Dolores Hidalgo to perform this ceremony.

Pamplonada

San Miguel de Allende (Third Saturday in September)

This is San Miguel de Allende's version of the Running of the Bulls in Pamplona, Spain. The bulls are released in front of the Parroquia and they run past the Templo San Francisco, returning to the Jardín Principal. The entire route is barricaded to prevent any bulls from getting loose in the town. The event attracts a large crowd of mainly young people and can be very dangerous.

Fiestas del Arcángel San Miguel
(Feast of Saint Michael the Archangel)

San Miguel de Allende (Weekend after September 29)

These festivities of the city's patron saint are the most important in San Miguel de Allende. They are also the most colorful and spectacular. The celebrations begin on Friday as people begin to pour in from the countryside. By nightfall, the Jardín Principal and the courtyard of the Parroquia are packed with people as mariachi bands play to the crowds. At 4 AM the next morning, tolling church bells ring in a fireworks display. This is traditionally supposed to be a very emotional event in honor of Saint Michael. Then the bands that have gathered play *Las Mañanitas*, the song that is best known as the traditional Mexican birthday song. That morning, the celebrants have tamales and *atole* (Mexican hot chocolate) for breakfast as the sun comes up. In the afternoon, a procession of indigenous Mexicans make their way through the Jardín Principal to the Parroquia in order to make offerings of *xuchiles*, beautiful braids of marigolds and colored tortillas.

The streets of Guanajuato get crowded during festivals.

The next day, a solemn mass is held in honor of Saint Michael, and the town pays homage to Friar Juan de San Miguel (founder of the city) with another parade.

Cerventino Festival

Guanajuato (Three Weeks in October)
This festival has come to be known as one of Latin America's most important cultural events. Certainly, it is the biggest thing to hit Guanajuato every year. During this celebration, thousands of fans of the 16th-century Spanish writer Miguel de Cervantes and his book Don Quijote make a pilgrimage to the city for three weeks of theater, dance, music, and literary events. The festival has its humble beginnings in the 1950s when students from the university took to the streets with performances of short works written by Cervantes known as entremeses. In 1972, it became an international festival celebrated throughout Latin America. However, its epicenter remains in Guanajuato, with artists from more than 30 countries giving performances during the festival. The main venues for these events are the city's theatres, such as Teatro Juárez, Teatro Principal—and of course,

Teatro Cervantes. However, a constant stream of events also takes place in the city's churches, plazas, and in the streets as well.

International Balloon Festival

León (End of November)

Over the course of four days the skies above León are filled with dozens of colorful hot air balloons as thousands of spectators gather to enjoy the events. Early in the morning in the city's Metropolitan Park these balloons begin their launches, filling the chilled air with the sound of the enormous blazes that heat the balloons. This magnificent scene is repeated throughout the day as the skies fill with multicolored globes. At night, the flames are ignited once again, creating a spectacle of giant lanterns. However, the festival is about more than balloons. The four-day event is jam-packed with other exhibitions, presentations, and performances—including live music concerts, BMX bike exhibitions, and all kinds of diversions for the kids. For more information, visit their Web site at www.festivaldelglobo.com.mx.

Las Fiestas Navideñas

Guanajuato (Last Two Weeks of December)

Christmas is celebrated with two full weeks of celebrations and solemn religious ceremonies. The *posadas* are performed throughout the region, in which processions of people leave church and reenact the journey of Joseph and Mary as they tried to find a place to stay on the night of Christmas Eve. This is a lively tradition, especially for children. Finally, at designated locations shelter is given to the pilgrims, where they receive *buñuelo* (sweet bread) and *atole* and children break piñatas. One of the most popular Christmas celebrations is held in San Miguel de Allende at the Nuestra Señora de Loreto next to the Templo Oratorio. Here, ancient chants can be heard and an extended mass is offered.

SUPERMARKETS

Guanajuato

Comercial Mexicana
473-732-9628
Avenida Juárez #131, Guanajuato, Gto. 36000
Open: Daily 8 AM–10 PM

Mega Comercial Mexicana
415-120-9047
Salida a Celaya and Libramiento Zavala Zavala, San Miguel de
Allende, Gto. 37700
Open: Daily 8 AM–10 PM

Super Gigante
415-120-9047
Libramiento Zavala Zavala and Carretera a Querétaro, San Miguel de
Allende, Gto. 37700
Open: Daily 8 AM–10 PM

WEATHER

If you're looking for a place with a temperate climate that you can
always count on, you've come to the right place. This region is famous
for its nice weather, typical of mountainous Central Mexico. Normally
from April through June temperatures peak out in the mid-80s during
the daytime, though daytime temperatures have been known to creep
up into the high 90s in May and June. The dry mountain air makes
this tolerable, and cool mountain breezes make the evenings wonderful during this time, when temperatures typically remain in the high
50s. The evenings can get quite chilling from November through
February. San Miguel de Allende is at 6,400 feet and Guanajuato is
almost at 6,600 feet, and temperatures fall down into the mid-40s at
night—even freezing overnight during the peak winter weeks. However, things tend to warm up quite quickly when the sun comes up,
with daytime temperatures typically rising into the low- to mid-70s. If
you are coming from Canada or the midwestern United States, these
temperatures will likely prompt you into shorts and a T-shirt while
you will see locals walking about bundled in sweaters and jackets. Just
remember that the temperature drops when the sun goes down, so
dress in layers.

The rainy season lasts from June to September and usually comes
in the form of late afternoon and evening showers. If you're out and
about at this time, bring an umbrella and be prepared to duck into a
coffee shop to wait out the shower. Rainfall typically averages around
4 to 5 inches a month during this period. In fact, these quick showers
can flood the streets, making you realize exactly why the sidewalks are

abnormally high. For the most part, however, the weather is perfect for sightseeing, kicking back by the pool, or taking a long afternoon nap.

The high season for tourists lasts from December 15 to April 1, when days are sunny and clear and nights are crisp and cool. The low season lasts during the hotter days of April through August. However, the city gets particularly crowded during Holy Week before Easter. This is when visitors from all over Mexico go on vacation to traditional places like San Miguel de Allende, where the festivities and processions are among the best in all of Latin America.

WHAT TO BRING

Obviously, if you are traveling to Guanajuato, San Miguel de Allende, or Dolores Hidalgo, you are going to want to bring a camera and a comfortable pair of shoes. If you are going to visit during Christmas or soon thereafter, a jacket will certainly be a must. These towns are located at a high altitude and they tend to get cold at night. Two other items that you'll need if you plan on touring around are sunscreen and a roll of toilet paper. The sunscreen is obvious. The high altitude and the dry, sunny air can combine to wreak havoc on your skin. As far as the toilet paper goes, some off-the-beaten-path restrooms will charge you a few pesos and give you a couple of squares—but in some places there just *isn't* any. Better to come prepared than find yourself in a situation where you have to improvise. Additionally, you'll want to have a tube or bottle of disinfectant hand lotion or disinfectant wipes to freshen up with. This comes in handy in a variety of situations.

One saying seems to have gotten truer in recent years: There are two types of luggage—carry-on luggage and lost luggage. We all know people who have taken trips and ended up spending days waiting for their luggage to arrive at their destination. It's best to pack light and carry all of your belongings aboard with you as you make your way south. But this is not always a possibility. A good trick is to make arrangements with your hotel and ship your belongings ahead. This costs extra, of course, but the peace of mind that it buys is really priceless.

Index

A

Abue Restaurante (Guanajuato), 137
Acadamia Falcon (Guanajuato), 182
Academia Hispano Americana (San Miguel), 45–46, 113
accommodations: bathrooms and toilet paper, 76–77; Guanajuato, 121, 123–33; prices, 15, 17; San Miguel de Allende, 69–86
Adventure Mexican Insurance, 56
Aeropuerto del Bajio (BJX), 50–51
Aeropuerto Internacional de Querétaro (QRO), 51
air travel (airlines, airports), 50–51
Alamo Car Rental, 60
Alcázar Hotel (San Miguel), 71
alebríjes, 99, 155
Alfaro, Luis Felipe Neri de, 110, 197
Alfredo Dugés Natural History Museum (Guanajuato), 168
Alhóndiga (Guanajuato), dining, 145–47
Alhóndiga de Granaditas (Guanajuato), 41, 163–64
Alkatraz (Guanajuato), 150–51
Allende, Ignacio, 37–38, 40–41, 74–75, 105, 187
ambulance: Guanajuato, 205; San Miguel de Allende, 206
Angela Peralta Theater (San Miguel), 46, 105
Antigua Villa Santa Mónica (San Miguel), 81–82

Apple (Guanajuato), 154
archaeological collection, at Museo de la Alhóndiga de Granaditas (Guanajuato), 163–64
archaeological site: Santuarío Cañada de la Virgen, 200
architectural heritage: Guanajuato, 157–63; San Miguel de Allende, 102–3. See also churches and cathedrals; Churrigueresque
Arcos del Atascadero B&B (San Miguel), 118
art classes, in San Miguel de Allende, 115–17
art galleries, in San Miguel de Allende, 105–8
art museums, in Guanajuato, 165–68
art tours, 119
artists' colony, birth of, 43–47
arts and crafts. See handicrafts
arts and culture: Guanajuato, 163–83; San Miguel de Allende, 105–13
Atención San Miguel (newspaper), 219
ATM machines, 217
Atotonílco, 37, 197–98; lodging, 85–86
Atotonílco el Viejo Hotel Resort & Spa, 85–86
Atotonílco Sanctuary, 197–98
ATVs, 59, 119
auto travel. See car travel
Avis Rent a Car, 60

B

B Lounge (Guanajuato), 154
Bacara (San Miguel), 96
Bagel Cafetín (Guanajuato), 138
baile folklórico dancers, 177
bakeries, 89, 92
Balloon Festival (León), 228
balloon rides, in San Miguel, 119
Banamex, 206
Bancomer, 207
banks, 206–7
Banorte, 206–7
Bar Fly (Guanajuato), 151
Bar Leonardo (San Miguel), 94
Bar Ocho (Guanajuato), 149–50
Barrera, Gabriel de la, 173–74
bars: Guanajuato, 148–54; San Miguel
    de Allende, 94–96
Basilica Colegiata de Nuestra Señora
    de Guanajuato, 175–77
bathroom etiquette, 76–77
beggars (begging), 220–21
Bellas Artes (San Miguel), 116
Berlin (San Miguel), 94
biking, 119, 199, 203
birds (bird-watching), 22, 85, 199,
    202, 203
Bora Bora Micheladas and Food
    (Guanajuato), 150
border crossing, 57–59
Border Crossings (San Miguel), 215
Bossanova Crêperia Café (Guanajua-
    to), 142–43
botanical gardens, 26, 199
Botica Agundis (San Miguel), 219
Botica de Santa Teresita (San Miguel),
    219
Buenas Noches (San Miguel), 100
Bugambilia (San Miguel), 90–91
buses (bus travel), 51–52, 65, 207
Bustamante, Anastasio, 109

C

cabs, 59, 61
Café Atrio (Guanajuato), 136
Café Conquistador (Guanajuato), 147
Café del Jardín (San Miguel), 87
Café El Midi (Guanajuato), 144
Café Etc. (San Miguel), 211
Calle Positos (Guanajuato), dining, 147
Callejón del Beso (Guanajuato), 157,
    159
Camébaro, 203
Camila (San Miguel), 98
camping, 185, 199, 202, 203
Cañada de la Virgen, 200; map, 201
Canadian Embassy, 205
Cantinala Coronela (San Miguel), 95
Capitolio (Guanajuato), 151, 154
car insurance, 55–56
car rentals, 59, 60
car travel (driving), 53–58; gas, 57;
    Guanajuato, 63–64; highways, 53;
    military stops, 56–57; at night, 54;
    San Miguel de Allende, 64–65;
    speed limits, 55; toll roads, 54–55
Caracol Collection (San Miguel), 99
Carretera Panorámica (Guanajuato):
    lodging, 129–32
Casa Azul (Guanajuato), 125–26
Casa Calderoni (San Miguel), 75–76
Casa Colorada (Guanajuato), 132
Casa de Aves (San Miguel), 85
Casa de Capelo (Guanajuato), 155
Casa de la Cuesta (San Miguel), 76–77
Casa de las Artesenias de Michoacán
    (San Miguel), 100
Casa de Líza (San Miguel), 80
Casa de Sierra Nevada Hotel (San
    Miguel), 79, 92
Casa del Parque (San Miguel), 92
Casa Diana (San Miguel), 78–79
Casa Linda (San Miguel), 70–71
Casa Payo (San Miguel), 89
Casa Puesta del Sol (San Miguel),
    83–84
Casa Rosada (San Miguel), 72
Casa Schuck Boutique Hotel (San
    Miguel), 84–85
Castillo de Santa Cecilia (Guanajuato),
    129–30
Cave Day (Guanajuato), 225–26
Celebrations San Miguel, 209
Centro Bilingue (San Miguel), 113
Centro Medico la Presa (Guanajuato),
    215–16

Centro Mexicano de Lengua y Cultura de San Miguel, 113–14
Cerro de la Bufa (Guanajuato), 184–85
Cerro del Cubilete, 196
Cerroblanco (San Miguel), 96–97
Cervantes, Miguel: Museo Iconografico del Quijote (Guanajuato), 169–70
Cerventino Festival (Guanajuato), 227–28
Chao Bella (Guanajuato), 147
Charco del Ingenio Botanical Gardens and Ecological Reserve, 26, 199
children, traveling with, 58–59; classes, 113–14, 117, 183; documents for entry, 57–59; restrooms, 77
Chimarrao (San Miguel), 92
Christmas festivities, 221, 228
churches and cathedrals: Atotonílco, 197–98; Dolores Hidalgo, 189–91; Guanajuato, 175–82; San Miguel de Allende, 108–13. *See also specific churches and cathedrals*
Churrigueresque, 103, 109–10, 167–68, 177–78, 181–82
Classes Unlimited (San Miguel), 117
climate, 229–30
climbing. *See* rock climbing
Collegiate Basilica of Our Lady of Guanajuato, 175–77
Colonial Guanajuato, 61–63, 121, 123, 157, 159; dining, 133–36; lodging, 123–29; map, 167; nightlife, 148–51
Comercial Mexicana (Guanajuato), 228
consulates, 206
cooking classes, in San Miguel de Allende, 117–19
Cook's Tour of San Miguel de Allende, 118–19
Corona Rally México (León), 222
Corondu (Guanajuato), 151
Cossío del Pomar, Felipe, 43–45, 116
Costa, Olga, 164, 167–68
Coyote Canyon Adventures (San Miguel), 119
crafts. *See* handicrafts
credit cards, 217

Cristo Rey del Cubilete, 196–97
Culinary Adventures of Mexico (San Miguel), 118
cultural differences, 195
cultural history, 27–47
currency and exchange, 216–19
customs regulations, 57–58
cybercafés, 210–12

D

dance clubs. *See* nightlife
De Wallen (Guanajuato), 149
Día de la Cueva (Guanajuato), 225–26
Dicambios Foreign Currency Exchange (San Miguel), 218
Dickinson, Stirling, 44, 45
Diego Rivera Museum (Guanajuato), 165–66
dining: Guanajuato, 133–47; San Miguel de Allende, 86–94
Divisas Dimas (Guanajuato), 217
documents for entry, 57–58
dogs, traveling with, 59
Dolce Capriccio (San Miguel), 88
Dolores Hidalgo, 187–93; events, 226; history of, 27, 37–38, 40–41; ice cream, 190–91; map, 188
Dolphy (San Miguel), 88
Don Ignacio Allende Dam, 22–23
Don Quixote Iconographic Museum (Guanajuato), 169–70
Don Quixote statue (Guanajuato), 151, 170
Donkey Jote (Guanajuato), 155
Dos Casas (San Miguel), 80
driver's licenses, 57
driving. *See* car travel
drugstores, 219
Dugés, Alfredo, 168

E

earthenware. *See* talavera
Easter, 220–21, 223–24
Edina Sagert Studio (San Miguel), 117
El Abue Restaurante (Guanajuato), 137
El Alcázar Hotel (San Miguel), 71
El Buen Café (San Miguel), 92, 118

El Café Galería (Guanajuato), 133
El Campanero Bridge (Guanajuato), 159
El Caporal (San Miguel), 96
El Charco del Ingenio Botanical Gardens and Ecological Reserve, 26, 199
El Colibrí (San Miguel), 97–98
El Correo (San Miguel), 88
El Gallo Pitagorico (Guanajuato), 134–35
El Jardín de los Milagros (Guanajuato), 146
El Market Bistro (San Miguel), 92–94
El Nigromante (San Miguel), 116
El Pegaso Restaurant Bar (San Miguel), 88
El Pípila (Juan José de los Reyes Martínez Amaro), 159–61, 163–64
El Pípila monument (Guanajuato), 157, 159–61
El Rincón de los Sabores (Guanajuato), 146–47
El Rinconcito (San Miguel), 91
El Ring (San Miguel), 96
El Viejo Zaguán (Guanajuato), 154–55
electricity, 208
Elizondo, Fidias, 109
email, 210–12
embassies, 205
emergency services, 205–6
enchiladas mineras, 141, 146
Escuela Mexicana (Guanajuato), 182–83
Estación Internet (San Miguel), 211
estudiantina, 152–53
ETN, 52
events, 220–28
Exim (San Miguel), 96
Explora Science Center Museum (León), 194
Express Laundry (San Miguel), 214

F

families. See children, traveling with
Farmacia Guadalajara (San Miguel), 219
Farmacia Guanajuato (San Miguel), 219
Farmacia Isseg (Guanajuato), 219
Farmacia Regina (Guanajuato), 219
Farmacia San Francisco (Guanajuato), 219
Feast of Saint Michael the Archangel (San Miguel), 226–27
Festival de la Independencia (Dolores Hidalgo), 226
festivals, 220–28
Fiesta del Arcángel San Miguel (San Miguel), 226–27
Fiesta del Señor de la Conquista (San Miguel), 222
Fiestas Navideñas (Guanajuato), 228
Fiestas of San Juan and Presa de la Olla (Guanajuato), 224–25
Finca Home (San Miguel), 100
fire departments: Guanajuato, 205; San Miguel de Allende, 206
firearms, 56
fishing, 202
Flecha Amarilla, 52
Florencio Antillón Park (Guanajuato), 183–84
folk arts. See handicrafts
food. See cooking classes, in San Miguel de Allende; dining
Frascati (Guanajuato), 134
Friday of Sorrows (Guanajuato), 222–23
Friedeberg, Pedro, 78–79

G

Galería Arte Sacro (San Miguel), 107
Galería Mariposa (San Miguel), 98–99
Galería Pérgola (San Miguel), 107–8
galleries. See art galleries, in San Miguel de Allende
gasoline, 57
ghost town tours, 119
Gonzalez Tours and Transportation (San Miguel), 119
Gorky González Quiñones (Guanajuato), 155
greetings, 132, 212
Grumara (Guanajuato), 210
Guanajuato, 121–85; architectural heritage, 157–63; arts and culture,

163–83; banks, 206; buses, 51–52, 207; car rentals, 60; car travel, 53–55; currency exchange, 217; dining, 133–47; events, 220–28; history of, 27–47; information sources, 205; Internet access, 210–11; language schools, 182–83; laundry service, 214; lodging, 121, 123–33; mail, 215; maps, 122, 167, 178; medical services, 215–16; museums, 163–74; nightlife, 148–54; outdoor activities, 183–85; pharmacies, 219; sacred sites, 175–82; shopping, 154–56; supermarkets, 228; taxis, 61; theater, 174–75; tours, 185; transportation, 61–64
Guanajuato Grill (Guanajuato), 150
Guanajuato mines, 33, 171–73, 203
Guanajuato Mummies, 170–71
Guanajuato Office of Tourism, 185
Guanajuato Semidesert, 25–27
guided tours. *See* tours
Guitar Festival (San Miguel), 225
guns, 56
Gutiérrez, Zeferino, 27, 42, 103, 108–9, 111, 113

H

Hacienda de Barrera Grande (Guanajuato), 173–74
Hacienda de Guadalupe (Guanajuato), 167
Hacienda de las Flores (San Miguel), 79–80
handicrafts: Guanajuato, 154–56; San Miguel de Allende, 96–102
Hardy Spanish School (San Miguel), 115
Harry's New Orleans Café (San Miguel), 90
HBC, 206, 207
Hernández, Javier de Jesús, 155
Hertz Car Rental, 60
Hidalgo, Father Miguel, 37–38, 40, 159, 184, 187–89, 192–93; Museum (Dolores Hidalgo), 192
Hidalgo Market (Guanajuato), 156
hiking: El Charco del Ingenio, 199;

Guanajuato, 183–85; Sierra de Lobos, 202; Valle de Santiago, 203; Zona Recreativa de las Palomas, 203
Hispano-American Academy (San Miguel), 45–46, 113
history, 19–47; cultural, 27–47; natural, 21–27
Hola Rent a Car (San Miguel), 60
holidays, 220–28
Holy Week, 220–21, 223–24
horseback riding, 119, 185, 199, 200
Hospital Civil (San Miguel), 216
Hospital de la Fé (San Miguel), 216
Hospital General de Guanajuato, 216
hospitals, 215–16
Hotel Gran Plaza (Guanajuato), 132–33
Hotel La Abadia (Guanajuato), 129
Hotel Luna (Guanajuato), 124, 135–36, 148
Hotel Maria Cristina (Guanajuato), dining, 147
Hotel Paseo de la Presa (Guanajuato), 130
Hotel San Diego (Guanajuato), 123, 124, 134
hotels: bathrooms and toilet paper, 76–77; Guanajuato, 121, 123–33; prices, 15, 17; San Miguel de Allende, 69–86
Hugh Carpenter Cooking School (San Miguel), 118

I

ice cream: Dolores Hidalgo, 190–91; Guanajuato, 136
immigration, 57–58
Independence. *See* Mexican Independence
information sources, 205–7
Instant Mexico Auto Insurance, 56
Instituto Allende (San Miguel), 45, 107–8, 116–17
Instituto de Habal Hispana (San Miguel), 114–15
INTERCAM Casa de Cambio (San Miguel), 218

International Balloon Festival (León), 228

International Cerventino Festival (Guanajuato). *See* Cerventino Festival

International Guitar Festival (San Miguel), 225

Internet access, 210–12

Internet San Miguel, 211

Internet Station Y2K (Guanajuato), 211

J

Jardín Allende (San Miguel), 68–69; dining, 86–90; lodging, 69–74; shopping, 96–102

Jardín de la Unión (Guanajuato), 13, 121, 123, 177, 179; dining, 133–36; lodging, 123–25; nightlife, 148–51

Jardín el Cantador (Guanajuato), 127–28

Jiménez, José Alfredo, 21, 193

Juan Arturo Reyes Posada (Guanajuato), 211

Juan Ezcurdia Gallery (San Miguel), 108

Juárez, Benito, 39

K

Keith Keller's La Escuela (San Miguel), 117

Kelli Brown Jewelry (San Miguel), 101

Kesey, Ken, 46

kids, traveling with. *See* children, traveling with

L

La Alberca, 203

La Botellita (Guanajuato), 133–34

La Cañada de los Pajaritos, 25

La Capellina (Guanajuato), 138

La Capilla (San Miguel), 86–87

La Casa Azul (Guanajuato), 125–26

La Cava de la Princesa (San Miguel), 95–96

La Colmena Panadería (San Miguel), 89

La Estudiantina de la Universidad de Guanajuato, 152–53

La Finestra Caffé (San Miguel), 90

La Grotta (San Miguel), 92

La Gruta, 199–200

La Hoya de Cintura, 203

La Hoya de las Flores, 203

La Mansión del Bosque (San Miguel), 77–78

La Pila (San Miguel), 214–15

La Puertecita Boutique Hotel (San Miguel), 82–83

Lagundi (San Miguel), 97

Laja River basin, 21–23

language. *See* Spanish language

Las Colonias Dam, 199

Las Fiestas Navideñas (Guanajuato), 228

Las Leyendas (Guanajuato), 145

Las Mercedes (Guanajuato), 138

Las Musas (Guanajuato), 154

Las Palomas in La Cuenca de la Esperanza, 203

Las Terrazas San Miguel (San Miguel), 84

laundry service, 214–15

Lavandería Alfa (Guanajuato), 214

Lavandería Automatica Internacional (Guanajuato), 214

Lavandería El Reloj (San Miguel), 215

Lavandería Franco (San Miguel), 215

León, 194, 196; events, 222, 228

León Zoo, 194

liability insurance, 55–56

Libros el Tecolote (San Miguel), 98

LifePath Spa Retreats (San Miguel), 119

Limerick Pub (San Miguel), 94–95

live music. *See* music

lodging: bathrooms and toilet paper, 76–77; Guanajuato, 121, 123–33; prices, 15, 17; San Miguel de Allende, 69–86

Lord of the Conquest Feast (San Miguel), 222

Los Picachos Mountain Range, 23–25

Los Secretos (San Miguel), 209

Luna Bar (Guanajuato), 148

M

Mama Mia (San Miguel), 88–89, 94

Mansión del Bosque (San Miguel), 77–78

Mansion del Cantador (Guanajuato), 128–29

markets, in Guanajuato, 156

maps: Cañada de la Virgen, 201; Dolores Hidalgo, 188; Guanajuato, 122, 167, 178; San Miguel de Allende, 73

marriages in Mexico, 208–10

Martínez de Pocasangre, Miguel Antonio, 197

Martyrs' Square (León), 194

Mechicano's (San Miguel), 95

Medica Integral Guanajuatense, 216

medical services, 215–16

Mega Comercial Mexicana (San Miguel), 229

Mellado Horseback Riding (Guanajuato), 185

Mercado Hidalgo (Guanajuato), 156

Mesón de los Poetas (Guanajuato), 126

Mesón del Rosario (Guanajuato), 126–27

Mexican Independence, 36–38, 40–41, 105, 160–61, 163–64, 187–93

Mexican-Cooking Vacation (San Miguel), 118

Mexpro Mexican Auto Insurance, 56

micheladas, 94, 150

military stops, 56–57

mineral museum, in Guanajuato, 168

mines of Guanajuato, 33, 171–73, 203

Misión de los Angeles (San Miguel), 84

Monex (San Miguel), 218

money and money exchange, 216–19

Morado, José Chavez, 164, 167–68

Moto Rent (San Miguel), 60

mountain biking. *See* biking

Mummies of Guanajuato, 170–71

Museo Casa de Don Miguel Hidalgo (Dolores Hidalgo), 192

Museo Casa Diego Rivera (Guanajuato), 165–66

Museo de Arte Olga Costa-José Chavez Morado (Guanajuato), 167

Museo de Cera Guanajuato, 164–65

Museo de la Alhóndiga de Granaditas (Guanajuato), 163–64

Museo de la Independéncia Nacional (Dolores Hidalgo), 192–93

Museo de las Momias de Guanajuato, 170–71

Museo de Mineralogía (Guanajuato), 168

Museo del Pueblo de Guanajuato, 167–68

Museo Ex-Hacienda del Cochero (Guanajuato), 173

Museo Ex-Hacienda San Gabriel de Barrera (Guanajuato), 173–74

Museo Histórico de San Miguel de Allende, 105

Museo Iconográfico del Quijote (Guanajuato), 169–70

museums: Dolores Hidalgo, 192–93; Guanajuato, 163–74; San Miguel de Allende, 105. *See also specific museums*

music: Guanajuato, 123, 148–54, 224; San Miguel de Allende, 89, 91–92, 94–96, 116, 225

N

natural history, 21–27

natural history museum, in Guanajuato, 168

nature reserves, 202–3

Neveria y Mescelanea Siglo XXI (Guanajuato), 136

newspapers, 219

nightlife: Guanajuato, 148–54; San Miguel de Allende, 94–96

Nuestra Señora de Guanajuato, 175–77

Nuestra Señora de los Dolores (Dolores Hidalgo), 189–91

O

Oasis (San Miguel), 74

Olé-Olé (San Miguel), 91

Omnibus de Mexico, 52

Oratorio de San Felipe Neri (San Miguel), 110–11
organized tours. *See* tours

P

Pablo Suites (San Miguel), 81
packing tips, 61, 126, 230
Palomas in La Cuenca de la Esperanza, 203
Pamplonada (San Miguel), 226
panhandling, 220–21
Parangueo el Viejo, 203
Parish of Our Lady of Sorrows (Dolores Hidalgo), 189–91
Parque Acuatico Splash (León), 194, 196
Parque Benito Juárez (San Miguel), 77
Parroquia de Nuestra Señora de los Dolores (Dolores Hidalgo), 189–91
Parroquia de San Miguel (San Miguel), 108–9
Paseo de la Independéncia (Guanajuato), 185
passports, 57–59
PEMEX (Petroleos Mexicanos), 57
pets, traveling with, 59
pharmacies, 219
phones, 207
Pied Pipers of Guanajuato, 152–53
Piedras (San Miguel), 101–2
Pirinola II (Guanajuato), 141–42
Pizza Piazza (Guanajuato), 143–44
"Place of Frogs," 28–29
Plaza Allende (Guanajuato), 151, 170, 175
Plaza Civica (San Miguel), 74–75
Plaza de la Paz (Guanajuato), 125, 139, 175; dining, 139, 141; nightlife, 151, 154; shopping, 154–55
Plaza Principal (Dolores Hidalgo), 190–91
Plaza Reforma (Guanajuato), 145–46
Plaza San Diego (Guanajuato), 123
Plaza San Roque (Guanajuato), 181
Plazuela Baratillo (Guanajuato), 125; dining, 137–38

Plazuela San Fernando (Guanajuato), dining, 141–45
Polanco Tours (San Miguel), 119
police: Guanajuato, 205; San Miguel de Allende, 206
Posada Carmina (San Miguel), 72–73
Posada Corazón (San Miguel), 73–74
Posada de las Monjas (San Miguel), 74
Posada de San Francisco (San Miguel), 69–70
Posada Santa Fe (Guanajuato), 124–25
post offices, 215
pottery. *See talavera*
poverty in Guanajuato, 220–21
Pozos, 119
Presa de Allende Reservoir, 200
Presa de la Olla (Guanajuato), 183–84; festival, 224–25
prices, 15, 17
Primera Plus, 52
Productos Herco (San Miguel), 96
Pueblo Viejo (San Miguel), 88
Puerta del Sol (Guanajuato), 151
Punto G (San Miguel), 212

Q

Quinta Las Acacias (Guanajuato), 130

R

Real de Minas Guanajuato, 33, 171–72
Red Cross, 206
Restaurante Conde Rul (Guanajuato), 135–36
Restaurante Teresita (Guanajuato), 147
restaurants: Guanajuato, 133–47; San Miguel de Allende, 86–94. *See also specific restaurants*
restroom etiquette, 76–77
Rincón de Don Tomás (San Miguel), 86
Rincón de los Sabores (Guanajuato), 146–47
Rivera (Diego) Museum (Guanajuato), 165–66

rock climbing, 184–85, 199, 202
Romano's (San Miguel), 94

S

sacred sites: Dolores Hidalgo, 189–91; Guanajuato, 175–82; San Miguel de Allende, 108–13
Saint Michael the Archangel Feast (San Miguel), 226–27
Saint Michael the Archangel Parish Church (San Miguel), 108–9
Saint's Feast Day, 224–25
San Agustín Café (San Miguel), 87–88
San Antonio de Padua (San Miguel), 225
San Diego Church of Alcántara (Guanajuato), 152–53, 177, 179
San Francisco Church (Guanajuato), 179, 181
San Francisco Church (San Miguel), 109–10
San Juan Festival, 224–25
San Miguel de Allende, 67–119; architectural heritage, 102–3; art classes, 115–17; art galleries, 105–8; arts and culture, 105–13; banks, 206–7; buses, 51–52, 207; car rentals, 60; car travel, 53–55; cooking classes, 117–19; currency exchange, 218; dining, 86–94; events, 220–28; history of, 27–47; information sources, 206; Internet access, 211–12; language schools, 113–15; laundry service, 214; lodging, 69–86; mail, 215; map, 73; medical services, 216; museums, 105; nightlife, 94–96; pharmacies, 219; sacred sites, 108–13; shopping, 96–102; supermarkets, 229; taxis, 61; tours, 119; transportation, 64–65; wedding planners, 209–10
San Miguel Designs, 101
San Miguel Weddings, 209
Santuarío Cañada de la Virgen, 200; map, 201
Santuarío de Atotonílco, 197–98
Santuarío de Mineral de Cata (Guanajuato), 181–82

seasonal events, 220–28
seasons, 229–30
Semana Santa, 220–21, 223–24
Serfin-Santander, 206, 207
Servicios Populares de Irapuat (Guanajuato), 217
shopping: Guanajuato, 154–56; San Miguel de Allende, 96–102
Sierra de Lobos Nature Reserve, 202
Sierra Nevada Hotel (San Miguel), 79
silver mines of Guanajuato, 33, 171–73, 203
Sollano 16 (San Miguel), 98
Solutions (San Miguel), 215
Spanish language, 195, 212–14; helpful phrases, 213–14; quick tips, 68, 102, 132, 212
Spanish language schools: Guanajuato, 182–83; San Miguel de Allende, 113–15
Subida del Tecolote (Guanajuato), 159
Super Gigante (San Miguel), 229
supermarkets, 228–29
Surfaces (San Miguel), 99–100
Susurro (San Miguel), 81

T

talavera, 96, 98, 99, 155
Tapas y Tinis (San Miguel), 95
Tasca de la Paz (Guanajuato), 139, 141
taxis, 59, 61
Teatro Angela Peralta (San Miguel), 46, 105
Teatro Cervantes (Guanajuato), 175
Teatro Juárez (Guanajuato), 174
Teatro Principal (Guanajuato), 174–75
telephones, 207
Templo de la Compañía de Jesús (Guanajuato), 182
Templo de la Concepcion (San Miguel), 111, 113
Templo de los Hospitales (Guanajuato), 179
Templo de Nuestra Señora de la Salud (San Miguel), 110
Templo del Inmaculado Corazón de María (Belén) (Guanajuato), 181

Templo San Diego de Alcántara (Guanajuato), 152–53, 177, 179
Templo San Francisco (Guanajuato), 179, 181
Templo San Francisco (San Miguel), 109–10
Templo San Roque (Guanajuato), 181
Terrazas San Miguel (San Miguel), 84
theater: Guanajuato, 174–75; San Miguel de Allende, 105
thermal springs, 199–200, 203
Tic Tic (Guanajuato), 146
tickets, 49
Tío Lucas (San Miguel), 91–92
tipping, 218–19
toilet paper and bathrooms, 76–77
toll roads, 54–55
torture museum, in Guanajuato, 173
tourist cards, 57–58
tours (tour companies): Guanajuato, 185; San Miguel de Allende, 119
Traditional Mexican Cooking School (San Miguel), 119
transportation, 49–65; around Guanajuato, 61–64; around San Miguel de Allende, 64–65; to Mexico, 49–55
Transportes del Norte, 52
Tunel de la Cuajín, 62
Tunel de los Ángeles, 184

U

UNESCO world heritage site. *See* Colonial Guanajuato
Universidad Autónimo de Guanajuato, 161–63, 168
U.S. Consulate, 206
U.S. Embassy, 205

V

Valenciana Mine (Guanajuato), 36, 171–73
Valle de Santiago, 203
Van Gogh (Guanajuato), 148–49
Vasco de Quiroga, 32, 179
Viernes de Dolores (Guanajuato), 222–23
Villa Maria Cristina (Guanajuato), 130–31
Villa Mirasol Hotel (San Miguel), 81
Villa Santa Mónica (San Miguel), 81–82
Virgin of Guanajuato, 177
volcanic craters, at Valle de Santiago, 203

W

walking. *See* hiking
War for Independence. *See* Mexican Independence
Warren Hardy Spanish School (San Miguel), 115
water park, in León, 194, 196
wax museum, in Guanajuato, 164–65
weather, 229–30
wedding planners, 209–10
weddings in Mexico, 208–10
Weddings San Miguel, 209–10
Why Not? (Guanajuato), 154
wildlife, 199, 203. *See also* birds
William Martin Gallery (San Miguel), 106–7

Z

Zaslavsky, Nancy, 118–19
Zócalo Mexican Folk Art (San Miguel), 99
Zona Recreativa de las Palomas, 203